Britain and the
First World War

Also from Unwin Hyman

THE BIRTH OF INDEPENDENT AIR POWER
British Air Policy in the First World War
Malcolm Cooper

BRITISH ECONOMIC AND STRATEGIC PLANNING,
  1905–1915
David French

BRITISH FOOD POLICY IN THE FIRST WORLD WAR
L. Margaret Barnett

BRITISH STRATEGY AND WAR AIMS, 1914–1916
David French

EUROPEAN ARMIES AND THE CONDUCT OF WAR
Hew Strachan

FIRE-POWER
British Army Weapons and Theories of War, 1904–1945
Shelford Bidwell and Dominick Graham

THE KILLING GROUND
The British Army, the Western Front and the Emergence of
  Warfare, 1900–18
Tim Travers

A STILLNESS HEARD AROUND THE WORLD
The End of the Great War: November 1918
Stanley Weintraub

WAR AND THE STATE
The Transformation of British Government, 1914–1919
Edited by Kathleen Burk

Britain
and the
First World War

Edited by

JOHN TURNER

Royal Holloway and Bedford New College
University of London

London
UNWIN HYMAN
Boston   Sydney   Wellington

Published by the Academic Division of
Unwin Hyman Ltd
15/17 Broadwick Street, London W1V 1FP

Allen & Unwin Inc.,
8 Winchester Place, Winchester, Mass. 01890, USA

Allen & Unwin (Australia) Ltd,
8 Napier Street, North Sydney, NSW 2060, Australia

Allen & Unwin (New Zealand) Ltd
in association with the Port Nicholson Press Ltd,
60 Cambridge Terrace, Wellington, New Zealand

First published in 1988

British Library Cataloguing in Publication Data

Britain and the First World War.
1. World War, 1914–1918—Great Britain
I. Turner, John,   *1949 May 18–*
940.3'41   D546

ISBN 0–04–445108–3
ISBN 0–04–445109–1 Pbk

Library of Congress Cataloging in Publication Data

Britain and the First World War/edited by John Turner
167p. 21cm.
Bibliography: p. 146
Includes index.
ISBN 0-04-445108-3 (alk. paper). ISBN 0-04-445109-1 (pbk. :
alk. paper)
1. World War, 1914–1918—Great Britain
I. Turner, John,   *1949 May 18–*
D546.B75 1988
940.3—dc19

Typeset in 10 on 11 point Times Roman
at Royal Holloway and Bedford New College,
and printed in Great Britain by Billing and Son,
London and Worcester

Contents

List of Maps

Source: Martin Gilbert, *First World War Atlas* (London: Weidenfeld & Nicolson, 1970)

List of Tables

Preface

Our aim in this book is to introduce students to the results of modern historical research on the British experience in the First World War. Each chapter gives a concise account of its subject, which will enable the reader to start exploring the mass of primary and secondary writing about the war which has been published since the Armistice on 11 November 1918. Many of the chapters were first developed as contributions to a conference for undergraduates and sixth-formers held at Royal Holloway and Bedford New College in March 1986, organized by the undergraduate History Society, and were later refined after discussions among some of the participants. Each author has also made suggestions for further reading in both secondary and accesible primary sources, which have been consolidated at the end of the book. Maps and tables have been used freely where they advance the argument, and readers are urged to use the lists on pages x–xii for cross-reference.

We are glad to thank the author and publishers for permission to reproduce maps from Martin Gilbert, *First World War Atlas* (London: Weidenfeld & Nicolson, 1970), which were drawn by Arthur Banks. The conference which was the first 'test-bed' for the book was organized with efficiency and style by the History Society of Royal Holloway and Bedford New College, led by James Pullé, Patricia Hawkins and Paul Symonds. I am grateful to all the contributors for producing their chapters on time, to length and in good order – a most unusual experience for the editor of a collective work.

JOHN TURNER

Royal Holloway and Bedford New College   July 1987

Introduction

JOHN TURNER

THE LOCOMOTIVE OF HISTORY?

The European war which began on 29 July 1914, and which Britain joined on 5 August, was widely expected to be over within a few months. It was a war between two major alliances whose hostility had been cultivated through more than a decade of diplomacy. It followed an arms race lasting more than two decades between Britain and Germany, whose competition in battleships had matched their commercial rivalry. Most British leaders expected that the Royal Navy would impose a successful blockade, while Britain's French and Russian allies would throw back and then crush the German and Austrian armies. Their German counterparts expected that a swift and devastating thrust through Belgium would knock France out of the war. The victorious Central Powers would then turn their attention to the Russian armies, which would also succumb to the superior generalship, better training and more powerful equipment of Germany and her Austrian allies.

It was not to be. Fifty-one months and about 9 million deaths later, the war was concluded. It was the first conflict since the Napoleonic wars to involve all the European powers, and the first major war to be fought with the full benefit of mechanized transport and mass-produced weaponry. All the industrial powers of the world had become involved. Japan and the United States had joined the Franco-British *entente cordiale*. Turkey had fought for four years on the German side, while Germany's erstwhile Italian allies had fought from May 1915 on the side of the Entente. At the end of the war Germany, Austria and Turkey all lost their empires and parts of their metropolitan territories. The régimes which had brought them into the war also fell. The Tsarist government in Russia was overthrown in 1917, and at the end of that year Russia surrendered to the Central Powers. The spoils of war went to the Western victors, who gained territory and (Italy excepted) preserved their prewar forms of government.

Few would now deny that the First World War was a critical episode in Britain's long retreat from territorial and economic domination of the world, or that after 1918 the social and economic world of Edwardian and Victorian Britain was irretrievably lost. Yet the war's historical significance is still ambiguous and controversial. About ¾ million British subjects died in battle, just under 7 per cent of the male population between 15 and 49. By the end of the fighting Britain, which in 1914 had been one of the world's greatest creditor nations, owed nearly $5 billion to the United States. Ten years after the end of the war 40 per cent of British government expenditure went to servicing war debt. On the brighter side, Britain was among the victors, and dominated European diplomacy after the war. In 1919 the Empire was larger than ever before. The war injured most of the country's economic competitors even more than it damaged Britain, at least in the short term. Some of the social changes brought about by the war seemed beneficial or neutral in their effects: women won greater economic and political freedom, the state accepted new responsibilities for the welfare of its citizens, the working classes acquired a greater homogeneity and political solidarity, and the social and political dominance of the landed aristocracy was broken.

Although it took a little time for Britain's underlying weaknesses to become obvious after 1918, historians tend with hindsight to attribute those weaknesses to the war. The postwar economic boom collapsed in 1921, and the British economy had not truly recovered by the time the 1929 Wall Street Crash shook the foundations of the economic world. The burden of being a Great Power, defending the enlarged Empire while maintaining a diplomatic lead in Europe and sustaining a large navy at the same time, proved too much for a declining industrial nation. At home the prewar party system was disrupted by war, though the attempt to put it all back together again was not abandoned until after 1929. Some of the social changes of war, notably the greater part played by women outside the home, seemed to be reversed in the aftermath, only to be reinstated gradually in the 1920s and 1930s. The rapid expansion of state activity was checked as soon as the war was over, and the passion for restricting public expenditure dominated both social and economic policy in the interwar years.

That British politics and society were changed by the war was to be expected. That the country was vulnerable to the damaging effects of war, and yet unable to take full advantage of victory, is not surprising if the war is considered in a larger historical context. The prewar years had not been static. The Liberal Party, the most notable political casualty, was divided before the war and already faced the threat of competition from the Labour Party. Britain's staple export industries met growing international competition before 1914: economic growth was slow compared with that of Germany, France and the United States, and slow growth was reflected in a lack of technical or commercial innovation. The state had already begun to expand, partly under the influence of a reforming Liberal government in domestic affairs but also partly in response to international tension, which encouraged large defence expenditure and a new authoritarianism exemplified in the Official Secrets Act of 1912. Changes in the relationship between different classes in society were well under way. The decline of the landed aristocracy was already being reflected in the composition of both houses of Parliament as well as in the distribution of wealth. The industrial working classes were gradually becoming more homogenous because of the breakdown of skill differentials under the influence of technological change. Popular culture in the late Victorian period had already begun to create a distinctive and self-confident working class. Although contemporaries understandably regarded the war as a deluge which swept away everything in its path,[1] it was in fact a deluge which closely followed the established course of change.

THE COURSE OF WAR

This is not a book about military history in the narrow sense: but the story of the fighting is not only the key to the war's abiding symbolic importance in twentieth-century history, but also the background to this book's main arguments. The peculiar horrors of trench warfare set the war on the Western Front apart from other conflicts in British historical consciousness. The campaign on the Somme in 1916 and the Third Battle of Ypres – Passchendaele – in 1917 stand out for their bloodiness and their manifest futility. In both offensives the British army attacked well-fortified trench positions with the help of heavy artillery fire. Strategic gains were very small, and casualties among the infantry were very high, especially in the first days of the Somme campaign and in the last phase of the Passchendaele offensive. Those who survived bullet, shrapnel, gas, and high explosive shell could look forward, at Passchendaele, to death by drowning

1 The image gave a title to Arthur Marwick's pioneering social history of the war: Arthur Marwick, *The Deluge* (London: Macmillan, 1965).

in mud. An army composed largely of civilians submitted to this hell on earth with remarkable meekness. Unlike the French army, which was paralysed by mutiny in the spring of 1917, the majority of British troops remained obedient to their leaders until the end of the war. A few minor mutinies in bases to the rear of the lines and a groundswell of complaint after the Passchendaele campaign were the worst that the army authorities had to deal with. This widespread acceptance of danger and suffering was not simply the result of spontaneous patriotism. Military discipline in the British army was harsh, and recent research has shown that many soldiers were executed *pour encourager les autres*, often without satisfactory judicial procedures.[2] Relations between officers and men were often distant, if not actively hostile. Nevertheless, it was an army which on the whole went willingly to war for most of the war's duration.

The Western Front set up a barrier to communication between soldier and civilian which both sides evidently found it difficult to cross. The published casualty-lists were impossible to ignore, and the loss of family or friends made death immediate and real to the bereaved. But the image of war as a fundamentally clean and decent, if rather hazardous, activity was widespread among civilians. Returning soldiers found themselves unable to talk about the trenches to their families and friends.[3] Newspaper reporting from the Front was controlled by the military censors; a good deal of it was inspired directly by General Headquarters. To many journalists maintaining civilian morale was as important as telling the whole truth. Politicians, unusually privileged among civilians in being able to visit the Front in person, were also readily absorbed into the world of headquarters and the staff. As a result very few civilian sources for the period suggest any acquaintance with the squalid and deadly world inhabited by the common soldier and brought to life in autobiographical fragments after the war. When some awareness did reach a senior politician, the effect could be remarkable. In January 1916 David Lloyd George, then Minister of Munitions, visited the son of a fellow Welsh MP. The young man had been shot through the head and was partly paralysed and in great pain: he died a few

2 Anthony Babington, *For The Sake of Example: Capital Courts Martial 1914–18* (London: Secker & Warburg, 1983).
3 See D. Englander and J. Osborne 'Jack, Tommy and Henry Dubb: the armed forces and the working class', *Historical Journal*, vol. 21 no. 3 (1978); G. Dallas and D. Gill, 'The mutiny at Etaples Base in 1917', *Past and Present*, no. 69 (1975); Denis Winter, *Death's men: soldiers of the Great War* (London: Allen Lane, 1978); E.J. Leed, *No Man's Land* (Cambridge: Cambridge University Press, 1979).

days later. Lloyd George almost broke down after his visit, telling his mistress that 'I wish I had not seen him. I ought not to have seen him. I feel that I cannot go on with my work....I was not made to deal with things of war.'[4] Most politicians managed not to see such things, and went on with their work without a moment's regret. Lloyd George himself was soon recovered, and went on to press for more conscription and, in September 1916, for the 'knockout blow' against Germany. In December 1916 he became prime minister and led the ministry which was still in place when the war ended. The civilian will to victory was indispensable to the war effort.

Willpower was needed because the war obstinately refused to proceed as the British public and its political leaders hoped. The Liberal Cabinet which was in power on the outbreak of war decided, after some dithering, to send an expeditionary force to France. Even with its help, the French armies were unable to throw the Germans back. The battle on the Western Front subsided into its trenches in November 1914. The Cabinet, which had recruited Lord Kitchener as Secretary of State for War to lend prestige as well as professional knowledge to their management of the struggle,[5] tried to think of other ways to win the war. Kitchener set about recruiting a huge land army; the Admiralty under Winston Churchill made a plan to attack Turkey by landing at the Dardanelles; and the Chancellor of the Exchequer, Lloyd George, prepared to increase industrial production and began to make his case for fighting the Central Powers at points of weakness rather than on the Western Front. The re-opening of the campaigning season in the spring of 1915 put these efforts to their first test. An offensive on the Western Front failed: the soldiers blamed the government for its failure to provide enough ammunition. Conflicting aims and bad co-ordination between navy and army at the Dardanelles were reflected in early losses of ships. The First Sea Lord, Admiral Lord Fisher, resigned on the grounds that Churchill, his political master, had overridden his advice and endangered the fleet. The coincidence of Fisher's resignation and the 'Shells Scandal' brought down the Liberal Cabinet in May 1915. The war had claimed its first major political victim.

4 *Lloyd George: A Diary by Frances Stevenson*, ed. A. J. P. Taylor, (London: Hutchinson, 1971), p. 93.
5 In August 1914 the Prime Minister, Asquith, was doing the job of Secretary of State for War because the previous incumbent, J. E. Seely, had recently resigned. Kitchener, the commander-in-chief in Egypt, who was in London in August 1914, was appointed as a non-political figure. He was later described, with justice, as a 'great poster'. He was drowned on the way to Russia in June 1916, rather to the relief of his colleagues.

H. H. Asquith, who had been prime minister since 1908, was not a man to relinquish power easily. Although he was forced to take Conservative leaders into the new coalition Cabinet, he made sure that they did not take the major offices. Andrew Bonar Law, the Conservative leader, had to be content with the Colonial Office. But, although the Liberals retained an apparent hegemony in the Cabinet, they were forced to make important concessions to their new colleagues. No sooner had politicians realized that the short war they had expected was turning into a very long war than they were forced to confront the possibility that either civilians or soldiers would refuse to go on making the sacrifices required of them. Slowly, and haphazardly, the government began to organize the nation for war, taking control of the engineering trade and other war-related industries. The Conservatives were determined to introduce military conscription, and after fierce arguments in which Lloyd George and Churchill took the conscriptionist side the Cabinet introduced the first Military Service Act in January 1916. The demands of an industrial war and of the very large land army – a novelty which had not been anticipated in all the war planning before 1914 – put great stress on the supply of manpower, which had to be allocated carefully between the army and the civilian economy. Imports of food and raw materials, especially under a submarine blockade, were also at a premium, and supplies of most commodities for civilian consumption were restricted to some degree. After the autumn of 1916, when Germany's policy of unrestricted submarine warfare began to bite, there were real fears that food supplies would be inadequate. Within the coalition Cabinet, battle-lines were drawn between Conservatives who wanted to sacrifice everything to keep up the military pressure on Germany, and Liberals who (with the notable exception of Lloyd George) wanted to play a long hand and preserve the country's economic power.

While the soldiers were being shot, bombed and gassed on the Western Front, civilian workers were made to work longer hours and accept substantial restrictions on their freedom, while suffering food shortages, housing shortages, and for many groups of workers a violently fluctuating relationship between their wages and the cost of living. In 1916 the Conservatives and Lloyd George won the strategic argument in Cabinet, and gambled that by putting this pressure on the civilian economy, and allowing the commander-in-chief on the Western Front, Sir Douglas Haig, to take part in a major offensive which became the Somme campaign, the war could be brought to an end within the year. The gamble failed, and the country faced renewed warfare with supplies, and morale, greatly depleted. An important side effect had been to inflame political tensions. Personal relations within the Cabinet, especially between Lloyd George and some of his Liberal colleagues, were very bad. Many Liberal MPs had come to detest Lloyd George and suspect him of wanting to replace Asquith; while many Conservatives also wanted to see Asquith and most of his Liberal colleagues out of the way, so that the war could be fought with more determination. Trade unionists had begun to revolt against their leaders and reject the concessions made on their behalf to government and the employers. Resistance to conscription, and resentment that the status of skilled workers was being eroded by the introduction of women and semi-skilled male workers into the munitions factories, boiled over into damaging strikes. Civilian willpower was gravely tested.

The military and political failures of 1916 simply increased the turmoil. The forced evacuation of the Dardanelles in January 1916 was a humiliation in the face of the Turkish armies, which was then compounded by the surrender of General Townsend's forces at Kut-el-Amara, in Mesopotamia, in April. The Somme campaign, though claimed as a success in its early stages, failed to achieve decisive results. The Grand Fleet's encounter with the German High Seas Fleet at Jutland was not exactly a defeat; nor was it the victory which years of navalist propaganda had promised. But the campaign on the Eastern Front promised most and delivered least. Russian armies under Brusilov made huge advances and captured thousands of prisoners, persuading Romania to enter the war. Then Brusilov's offensive collapsed and, by December, Russian operations against the Central Powers were halted, while Romania was driven out of the war. Closer to home, while the Cabinet tried desperately to stay in control of the war effort, disaffected Irishmen staged a small rising in Dublin on Easter Monday, as though to prove that not all the intractable problems of the prewar years had gone away. The Easter Rising was suppressed with brutal ineptitude. Lloyd George was commissioned to find an acceptable political settlement, and almost succeeded by persuading Nationalists and Unionists to agree on a partition which would give Home Rule in the south and leave Ulster in the United Kingdom. When this was discovered by Conservatives in the Cabinet, the foundations of the Asquith Coalition were shaken by their wrath, and the scheme was quickly dropped.

Any government, especially a divided government, would have been vulnerable at the end of 1916. Asquith fell in December, to be replaced at the head of a new coalition by Lloyd George. The new government was dominated by Conservatives and committed, in principle at least, to new methods. Most of the government's leading members wanted to curb the power of the generals while extending the government's control over the civilian economy. The Lloyd George Coalition presided over a period of crisis in Britain's war effort. In the spring of 1917 widespread strikes in the munition areas coincided, unhappily for the government, with news of the overthrow of the Tsar in Russia. The hurriedly appointed Commissions on Industrial Unrest found that the industrial working class population was extremely disgruntled by many things, of which the high price of food was the most widely felt: but they also reported a growing movement for a negotiated peace. Lloyd George warned the army that they could not have as many recruits as they wanted, for fear of political unrest if the scope of conscription was much expanded. Civilian willpower was near to breaking point.

The struggle for strategic control between the generals and the civilian politicians in the War Cabinet now attained a new importance and a new intensity. Lloyd George, who had come to power because most MPs thought he was committed to war *à l'outrance*, was now determined to limit casualties and preserve the country's strength for a long campaign. Outflanked by the soldiers who were intent on fighting in Flanders in 1917, he renewed his efforts to control them by setting up the Supreme War Council, an inter-Allied body for strategic planning, in October 1917. In February 1918, after another manpower crisis, he contrived the dismissal of Sir William Robertson, the Chief of the Imperial General Staff, who was replaced by the more flexible General Sir Henry Wilson. Yet Sir Douglas Haig was immovable: his close relationship with the king was matched by the strong support of the Conservative back benches in the House of Commons, and by the readiness of the press to speak out for the soldiers against political interference. While Lloyd George and Haig battled about the establishment of a general reserve and the appointment of the French General Foch as a 'generalissimo' over all Allied forces in France, the German army prepared its last offensive, which was launched on 21 March 1918. The first attack broke through the British lines and threatened to engulf the Channel ports and thus cut the British army off from its lines of supply. In military terms, this was Britain's gravest hour.

The government acted immediately to send more troops to France. The scope of the Military Service Act was further extended, to include men up to 51 and, momentously, Irishmen. The Irish had been exempted from all previous conscription measures because it was assumed that Irish loyalties were already strained and that conscription would ruin any hope of a peaceful settlement of the Irish question. It was now thought that British working men would not tolerate further conscription unless Ireland was included. The old fear was proved right. The Irish Nationalist Party flung itself into the arms of the separatist movement, Sinn Fein. To persuade them to support the government, the War Cabinet offered Home Rule, to be introduced simultaneously with conscription. At this, the Conservative Party erupted, threatening its leaders with withdrawal from the Coalition.

The Lloyd George Coalition's worst political moment of the war came in early May, triggered by allegations from General Sir Frederick Maurice that Lloyd George had lied to the House of Commons about the number of recruits supplied to the Western Front in 1917. Conservatives, who had put up with Lloyd George for seventeen months despite his past record and his high-handed treatment of the generals, now threatened to unseat him because his Irish policy was the last straw. A defeat for the government would have meant a general election. Partly because of the grave military situation, but mostly because they realized that the despised Asquith was the only possible replacement for Lloyd George, the Conservative dissidents relented. The 'Maurice Debate' ended in a defeat for Asquith's motion of censure. It was a close run thing, and for the rest of the war the government was preoccupied by the need to consolidate its parliamentary position. While battle raged on the Western Front, party managers on both sides of the coalition stepped up their efforts to arrange a wartime election which would bring them a more tractable House of Commons.

In this way the course of battle itself had an influence on the consequences of war which went beyond what can be explained by the economic and social implications of an 'industrial war'. The alignment of parties had been determined by military events. Election preparations made by the Coalition parties included a deliberate plan to control the spread of the Labour Party and to reinforce the divisions within Liberalism, so that the Coalition government could stay in power with enough parliamentary support to hold its strategic and economic course. The Coalition tactics were to split the Liberal Party between Coalitionists and Asquithians, and to defeat the Labour Party by accusing it of faint-heartedness in the war, while competing to offer a generous social and economic programme to the electorate. The Irish Party was sacrificed, and with it the hope of controlled change in Ireland. Though politicians could not foretell the future, they could be sure after May 1918 that neither politics nor society would ever be the same again.

In the event, the election was just preceded by the Armistice. The tide of battle in France began to turn in July, with the long-awaited intervention of American troops[6] and the exhaustion of the German army. The minor battle of Hamel on 4 July, conducted by the British Fourth Army, was remarkable among Western Front battles for achieving most of its objectives nearly on schedule, with small loss of life. The Battle of Amiens, which was launched on 8 August, had a similar success; and in subsequent operations it became obvious that the German army was at last crumbling. For the first time, offensive operations on the Western Front began to lead to steady successes. During September and October, without ever achieving the breakthrough and cavalry attack which were the Holy Grail of Haig's strategic ambitions, the British and French armies pushed the Germans back on their defensive lines, taking thousands of prisoners, reducing enemy morale, and finally forcing the German chief of staff, Ludendorff, to concede the impossibility of his situation by resigning on 26 October. German will to resist had been broken, and the end of the war, together with the fall of the Kaiser's regime, was assured. Germany's other allies were also forced out of the war, and a general armistice was signed on the Western Front on 11 November.

THE AFTERMATH

Once the fighting was over it was all the more clear that there was no prospect of return to the prewar world. The election, which was called for 14 December, was merely the most immediate and obvious sign of change. The political map had been redrawn by the 1918 Representation of the People Act, which had also enfranchized all adult males and most women over 30. The incumbent party was a coalition of Conservatives with Lloyd George's remaining Liberal supporters. The opposition consisted of Asquith's Liberal supporters and the Labour Party, which had decided at the last moment not to join in the Coalition appeal; but Labour and opposition Liberals did not co-operate. The result was a massive victory for the Coalition, in which the popularity of Conservative candidates, even when standing against officially endorsed Coalition Liberals, was the most prominent feature. The new Parliament, dominated in atmosphere at least by the Conservative 'hard-faced men who looked as though they had done well out of the war',[7] backed a Coalition government

---

6 The United States joined the war in April 1917, but logistic delays and lack of training ensured that the American army played no part on the Western Front in 1917.

7 A phrase used by Stanley Baldwin to describe the new crop of Conservative MPs in 1918, and widely quoted.

which tried to grapple with the economic, diplomatic, and political problems left by victory.

In each of these areas the new government and its interwar successors were forced to redeem the hostages rendered to fortune during the war, while changes quite beyond the control of governments made it impossible to return to 'normalcy'. The massive re-organization of the labour force had to be reversed. Demobilized soldiers had to be found jobs, and women persuaded to withdraw from the factories. Everyone expected 'decontrol' – the rapid abandonment of economic restrictions, especially on wages and prices, shipping and raw materials. Although some controls were abandoned in great haste, international shortages of shipping and raw materials forced the government to keep some of its powers. At the same time many politicians, especially Christopher Addison, who had been Minister of Reconstruction since August 1917, and Eric Geddes, the railway executive who had held a variety of posts and finished the war as First Lord of the Admiralty, wanted to make permanent changes in the organization of the economy. Addison wanted to use the state's borrowing power to build houses 'fit for heroes to live in' and thus cure one of Edwardian Britain's major social problems. He also wanted to make the new Ministry of Health, of which he was the first head, a vehicle for the expansion of social services. Geddes wanted to exploit the opportunities for state intervention in the economic infrastructure, by establishing a state-backed transport system integrating railways, docks, and electricity supply. To complement these economic changes, the President of the Board of Education, H. A. L. Fisher, had already passed legislation to expand secondary-school provision, with an emphasis on continuing education to create a more skilled workforce.

On the face of it the Coalition manifesto had allowed for all this, and at first Geddes and Addison were given a clear run. But the reaction soon set in. Conservative backbenchers did not like the 'socialistic schemes' put before them. Addison was at first supported by his Cabinet colleagues, who wanted the housing programme to help them head off social unrest, but when the collapse of the postwar boom weakened the trade union movement this lost its relevance, and Addison, whose plans had become very expensive, was sacrificed in 1921.[8] Geddes was never even allowed to develop his 'confiscatory' proposals in full in the face of backbench Conservative revolts. On the other hand, although tariff protection was very

8 On the politics of housing see Mark Swenarton, *Homes Fit for Heroes*, (London: Heinemann Educational Books, 1981).

popular on the Conservative back bench and among important ministers, Coalition Liberals would not stand for it. It was therefore impossible to get agreement on any positive effort in economic policy. The government was able to pass some protective legislation, such as the Safeguarding of Industry Act, the Dyestuffs Act and the Trade Facilities Act, but all of these were deliberately limited in their scope.

The effect of the slump was to reinforce pressures towards retrenchment, and especially to encourage deflationary monetary policies. This eventually led to the general assault on state expenditure known as the 'Geddes Axe': Sir Eric Geddes was called out of political retirement in 1922 to chair an advisory committee on public expenditure, which recommended cuts in expenditure. The housing programme, the education policy and even the remains of Geddes's own transport policy were ruthlessly cut down. The reasoning behind the committee's proposals was simple enough, and it illustrates how little the war had changed economic understanding. In 1914 Britain's monetary policy had been based on the Gold Standard: pounds sterling could be exchanged freely for gold at a fixed exchange rate which set the pound equal to US$4.86. Most major European currencies were similarly fixed. During the war the country had been forced 'off gold', and the import and export of gold had been forbidden. The exchange rate against the dollar had been allowed to slip. At the end of the war the pound stood at $4.76. Every British banker, and every responsible politician and civil servant believed that a 'return to gold' at the prewar parity was essential to prosperity. The Gold Standard was believed to be a perfect self-regulating mechanism, by which the economy of a country would be kept in balance. If sterling prices rose in a boom, so that British goods cost too much abroad, investors would exchange pounds for gold. To prevent a run on the gold reserves, the Bank of England would raise its interest rate. Other banks would follow, and the general increase in British interest rates would force British businessmen to curtail their activities. This would check the boom, prices would drop, and all would be well again. The magical effects of this mechanism could be enjoyed without any intervention by the government, merely by the operation of the market.

It was impossible to return to gold immediately after the war, but a string of advisory committees insisted that it was essential to do so as soon as possible, and that the first step must be to restrict the tax burden created by public expenditure, and to shift capital spending away from government activity. It was also important to control wages, so that British prices would approach those of the world market. Geddes was merely giving this policy a concrete form. In due course, in 1925, a Conservative government felt able to return to gold. Prosperity did not result, and the Gold Standard was abandoned once again in 1931; but no British government between the wars rejected the main plank of Geddes's argument. Outside the Liberal Party, which never regained power, and the back benches of the Labour Party, which never had much influence on Labour cabinets, no politician, civil servant or publicist of any substance doubted that for economic recovery to take place British wages must be cut to enable British staple industries to compete in a depressed world market, while public expenditure must be kept to a minimum.

War had also cast its shadow directly over socio-economic change. As soon as the postwar boom collapsed it was obvious that the staple industries were the worst hit. Over-capacity and shrinking markets, both brought about directly by war, destroyed the prosperity of ship-building, coal, cotton and steel. ' New' industries, stimulated by the technological demands of war, were not enough to compensate for depression in the staples, and by 1929 economists were talking of the 'intractable million' unemployed in the older industrial areas. Yet, except for the years of the Great Depression, between 1929 and 1932, the interwar period saw the British economy growing more strongly than before 1914, and more strongly than that of many of her industrial competitors, notably Germany, who had been worse hit by the war. Productivity also grew fast, partly because of improvements in production methods and organization which had been stimulated by the war. The combined effect of growth in some sectors and retardation in others was to shift the geographical and sectoral balance of the economy towards the Midlands and the South-east.

This development, and its direct links with war, can also be appreciated in human terms. The loss of life in Britain was proportionately less than in France or Germany, and much of the loss to Britain was compensated by the cessation of emigration during the war. These considerations were not important to a community mourning a 'lost generation', but the demographic consequences of war were not in fact very large in aggregate. In the interwar years, as a result, the consequences of nineteenth-century changes in population patterns reached maturity. Families grew smaller, a steadily increasing proportion of the population lay between the ages of 15 and 64, the 'occupied population', and there was correspondingly a smaller proportion of children and old people: in the jargon of welfare economics, the 'dependency ratio' was lower than in Edwardian times. This had profound consequences. At a time when the occupied population was proportionately at its largest, the economy was unable to provide enough jobs: this was why women were urged out of the labour force after the war. Traditional industrial areas were least affected by war casualties, because more of their manpower worked in protected industries during the war, and in those very areas the economic changes induced by war reduced employment opportunities most severely. Yet this unavoidable unemployment coincided with a productive period in the history of the British economy, brought about in part by the large proportion of the population which was available for productive work. For those in work and, because of the social welfare system, for many of those out of work too, the interwar period saw a growth in living standards which was especially marked after 1930.[9] In 1929, just before the Wall Street Crash, 5.6 per cent of insured workers were unemployed in London, against 13.5 per cent in northern England. This above all was a consequence of the war, which selectively left its blighted legacy over the most vulnerable parts of the country.

The postwar coalition did not attempt the same crude reversion to prewar policies in diplomacy as it had done for the domestic economy, nor would the changed balance of power have allowed it to do so. The most urgent need at the Paris Peace Conference was to reach a settlement of European boundaries which would satisfy the French desire for security, the British desire for a stable international system, and President Woodrow Wilson's conscience. The other problem was to contrive a policy for reparations to be paid by Germany which would satisfy British, French and American wishes. Lloyd George's difficulties at the conference stemmed mostly from his conduct of the election campaign, which had degenerated into an orchestrated demand to squeeze Germany 'until the pips squeaked'.[10] On the morrow of the election this was seen to be a bad policy, which threatened to disrupt the European economy, depending as it did on German prosperity, and also to make it quite impossible to reach a stable territorial settlement. Lloyd George had Clemenceau, one of France's most aggressive and successful politicians, at his front and the Conservative Party at his back; he also had to deal with Woodrow Wilson, whose public commitments to democracy and the principle of national self-determination were hard to match with the realities of Eastern Europe after the collapse of the Habsburg monarchy.

9 D. H. Aldcroft, *The Inter-War Economy: Britain, 1919–1939* (London: Batsford, 1970), pp. 352, 364.
10 This was in fact Geddes's phrase, but the decision to focus the campaign on retribution against Germany was taken by Lloyd George's aides.

The Treaty of Versailles, signed on 28 June 1919, was not quite a peace which passed all understanding, but it had few friends in Britain. Progressives, notably J. M. Keynes, criticized it for its vindictiveness towards Germany. Conservatives objected to the birth of a supranational League of Nations with a Covenant which seemed to limit British sovereignty, and they objected still more when the United States, whose president had dreamed it up, refused to join in 1920. British foreign policy after Versailles was mostly devoted to correcting the mistakes of 1919. Lloyd George and the Foreign Office pursued different and sometimes contradictory policies, with the general aim of bringing Germany back into the fold both politically and economically.

Two side-issues did considerable damage to British foreign policy immediately after the war. After the Bolshevik government of Russia had made peace with Germany with the Treaty of Brest-Litovsk in January 1918, British troops had been sent to Russia, ostensibly to help anti-Bolshevik forces to fight the Germans. In practice British forces were trying to achieve the overthrow of the Bolshevik régime, and they continued the attempt for some time after the armistice had been signed with Germany. The military expedition was understandably resented by the Soviet government, and British efforts to restore peaceful relations were half-hearted. On the one hand, Britain supported the Poles with munitions during the Russo-Polish war of 1919–20; on the other hand, Lloyd George repeatedly tried to get Russian delegations to attend the series of territorial and economic conferences which took place between 1919 and 1922. He finally succeeded at Genoa in April 1922, whereupon the Russians and the Germans made a mutually advantageous military and economic pact at Rapallo, while the disagreements between Russia and the Western Allies – principally over Soviet responsibility for Tsarist debts and Allied compensation for the period of intervention – remained unsolved. The government's policy of reconciliation was unpopular with the Conservative Party, and helped to secure Lloyd George's downfall. Yet the earlier interventionist policy had elevated a military side-show into a major problem of foreign policy. Russian hostility towards the Western Allies prevented diplomatic co-operation in the 1930s, was hardly abated during the Second World War, and survived to determine the pattern of international relations into the 1980s. This was a high price to pay for the slim chance of reviving a non-Bolshevik government in Russia in the immediate aftermath of the First World War.

The other, more minor side-show was Greece, and here the divergence between Lloyd George's own policy, implemented through his private secretariat, and the Foreign Office's policy, carried out by the Foreign Secretary himself, was more important. In brief, Lloyd George, even more than the Foreign Office, was a passionate supporter of the Greeks in their continuing battle with Turkey for the control of Thrace and Western Anatolia. The collapse of the Ottoman regime after the loss of its empire allowed Kemal Atatürk's nationalist movement to establish itself as a modernizing force in the Turkish heartland. By supporting the Greeks, Lloyd George's government found itself near to war with Atatürk's forces in October 1922. Withdrawal, though inevitable, was none the less undignified and did no good either to the government or to Britain's international standing.

Britain's main postwar problems, though, were not in Russia or Turkey, but in Europe and east of Suez. Having fought a war in alliance with France, and having fought it very largely to conform with French needs, Britain found it almost impossible to co-operate with French policy towards Germany, especially after France occupied the Ruhr in January 1923 to punish the Germans for defaulting on reparations payments. French hostility delayed the entry of Germany into the League of Nations, and also made it difficult to agree on a settlement of the reparations question which would not cripple the German economy. Britain was thus frustrated in the attempt to appease Germany, and had scarcely more success in achieving a general disarmament. In 1933 fourteen years of German resentment finally brought Hitler to power, and the Nazi régime withdrew from the disarmament talks. The European economy had been devastated anew by the Great Depression. Preparations for the next war began in earnest. From the perspective of British European policy, this marked the point at which the First World War might as well not have been fought: all Britain's European war aims had been thwarted, and after winning the war the Entente allies had convincingly lost the peace.

In the wider world Britain found it impossible to sustain the economic burdens of defending an enlarged empire; and within three years of the end of the war the worldwide naval hegemony for which so much had been sacrificed was simply given away. The occasion was the Washington Naval Conference (November 1921 – February 1922). This was called to resolve potential conflicts in the Pacific basin between Britain, Japan and the United States. Before 1914, Britain had relied on the Anglo-Japanese treaties of 1902 and 1911 for naval support in the Pacific. Japanese expansion in China made this relationship unpopular in Australia, New Zealand and Canada, and the Americans were also at odds with Japan. The Washington

Conference was called to deflect the possibility of a naval arms race between Japan and the United States by reviewing the structure of Great Power alliances in the Pacific. The result was a Five-Power Treaty which allowed Britain, America, Japan, France and Italy to maintain capital ships in the proportions 5 : 5 : 3 : 1.75 : 1.75, while the Anglo-Japanese treaties were not renewed. This was a far cry from the two-power standard to which British governments had aspired before 1914, which aimed for a navy to match the total strength of any two foreign navies. A greater irony was that in 1927, during a conference on the limitation of cruiser strengths, the British government brought talks to a standstill by insisting on an upper limit for the British fleet which would enable them to police the globe; but even after the talks broke down there was no attempt to build so many cruisers because the Cabinet would not spend the money. The problems of policing the empire, described by A. J. Stockwell in Chapter 2 below, led to military embarrassment and a steady erosion of power, as Britain was compelled to move, with as much dignity as could be summoned, towards allowing greater autonomy to India and other dependent territories. Thus the economic, diplomatic and strategic consequences of war were hardly what British leaders had wanted when they entered the conflict, or even when they entered the peace conference. A war fought to preserve Britain's position in the world had instead made it impossible to return to prewar conditions.

In party politics the shadow of war was equally long, but not so obviously malign, except for Liberals. By 1922 the Conservative Party had tired of Lloyd George and his coalition. The desire to return to 'normal' party politics was irresistible, but the Liberal Party was by then so divided and the Labour Party so well established that prewar politics could never be reconstructed. Instead the Conservatives fought the 1922 general election unaided, and won 344 seats. The Liberals were divided between National or Lloyd Georgian Liberals who won 53 seats and Official or Asquithian Liberals, who won 62. Labour, with 142 seats, was now the second party and destined to remain so for the future as then foreseen. In December 1923, Stanley Baldwin, who had succeeded to the premiership in May, called an election which left his government in a minority. Asquith for the Liberals chose to put Labour with its 191 MPs into power, and the first, short-lived cabinet of Ramsay Macdonald took office. For nine months the new ministers tried to prove they were neither 'doctrinaires, intellectuals and cranks' nor 'the

slowest-witted folk...ever encountered'.[11] Whether or not they succeeded they lost the next election, despite increasing their share of
the popular vote from 30.7 per cent to 33.3 per cent. The Liberals slumped: the beneficiaries were the Conservatives, who won a
convincing majority and remained in office until 1929. By then the
Liberal Party was beyond redemption. Lloyd George had succeeded
to the leadership after Asquith's retirement in 1926, and ostensibly
reunited the party. He also used his substantial political fund to
assist party organization and to promote a series of policy studies
which made the Liberal manifesto for the 1929 election a document of unusual fertility and insight. But the voters had changed
their habits, and the 1929 election made Labour the largest party
at 287 seats, with the Conservatives holding 260 and the Liberals
trailing with 59. After helping in a very subordinate role to prop up
the Labour government between 1929 and 1931, the Liberals found
themselves in the 1931 National Government, squabbling with their
Conservative colleagues and between themselves. The trauma of
the Lloyd George Coalition was repeated on a smaller scale, and
divisions between National and Official Liberals brought the party
to its knees by 1935.

The fundamental reasons for Liberal downfall remain a matter of
dispute. The Liberals' policies, especially the proposals for economic regeneration embodied in the Yellow Book manifesto for
the 1929 election, were more sophisticated and more constructive
than their rivals' offerings. Yet electoral decline seemed inexorable.
Some historians like to blame Lloyd George, who deliberately split
the party in 1917 and, according to his detractors, persistently failed
to work for its reunion thereafter. Others argue that the party was
in any case unable to adapt itself to a postwar electorate which was
increasingly divided on lines of class. The two views are not incompatible, though their protagonists like to make them so. Whatever the
cause, the mere fact of Liberal decline was important to the Labour
Party, which was able to make itself a plausible party of government without resolving all its own divisions. After the 1918 election
Labour established a heartland of safe seats in mining and industrial
areas, corresponding to Conservative fortresses in the suburbs and
the south-east of England. Liberalism was strong in the south-west
but scattered elsewhere; and the former Liberal voters drifted to the
other parties. Between the wars, although the Conservative Party

---

11 The words of a normal Conservative politician, confronted with the possibility of a Labour Cabinet: John Vincent (ed.), *The Crawford Papers*
(Manchester: Manchester University Press, 1984), p. 489.

dominated electoral politics, the choice of government was usually determined by the volatility of the Liberal vote. The party whose job it was to capture and retain that vote had been mortally wounded by the war.

THE SHAPE OF THIS BOOK

This is a book about Britain's experience in the First World War. It has not been our purpose here to argue about whether the war had consequences, nor to enter the fascinating debate about its causes. Instead the contributors have set out to examine how the war itself shaped the process of change in Britain.

By concentrating on the war in this way, we can see purposeful action where the longer view merely sees aimless destruction. What seems in a long perspective to be ghastly ill-luck often turns out to be the natural consequence of fighting an industrialized war. For example, David French makes the point below that British strategy did make sense, though at first it might not seem so. The British army was forced 'to make war as we must, and not as we should like to'.[12] The same was true of the Royal Navy, the culmination of the greatest arms race the world had ever seen, which sailed up and down for two years before fighting an indecisive fleet engagement, then retired to concentrate on escort and anti-submarine duties. Yet the navy's main task of keeping the seas open for British commerce was achieved; and the army eventually won a victory on the Western Front at an enormous cost in casualties, munitions and money.

At home, British governments were faced with difficult economic choices. Inevitably they made decisions from month to month, and just as inevitably some of these decisions created as many problems as they solved. In the economic as well as the military sphere, the war had its own commanding logic. Only a few voices at the time, such as Lord Lansdowne in his famous letter in November 1917, spoke up for a negotiated peace which would end the war before victory ruined the nation. The majority of the population could see no alternative to outright victory, at whatever cost: politicians who shared this view made sure to encourage it. The sacrifice of long-term economic strength, and thus the loss of global power which ultimately depended on a strong economy, was the greatest, yet the least avoidable consequence of war. Most of the old heavy industries – steel, coal, shipbuilding, heavy engineering and heavy

12 Dardanelles Committee Minutes, 20 August 1915, Public Record Office, Cabinet Papers, CAB 42/3/16.

chemicals – were given a new lease of life by the war, only to find that postwar demand could not absorb the capacity of their new plant. By contrast the textile industries were forced to run down, restricting their exports simply to free labour for the army and for war-related production. After the war their customers had turned to other suppliers. The result was the same. After the war, and especially after 1921, all the staple industries were chronically depressed. This was foreseen, but could only have been avoided by measures which might well have led to defeat. To understand the dilemmas, and thus to understand the effect of war on Britain's long-term position, we must examine the wartime context.

Self-inflicted damage in other spheres can also be explained readily in the context of war. The Liberal Party was at first divided between those who were willing to sacrifice 'Liberal principles' for the war effort and those who clung to the doctrines of free trade, international peace, and freedom of conscience. Liberal loyalties were confused when the Conservatives entered a Coalition under Asquith in 1915. In due course the supporters of war were further divided, becoming followers of Lloyd George or followers of Asquith after December 1916. In the 1918 election the pro-war Asquithians and the early dissenters were reunited in an enfeebled opposition to the Lloyd George Coalition. Liberalism never recovered from these disasters. By contrast the Labour Party, divided on the same lines early in the war, preserved some harmony among its leaders and fought the 1918 election as a united party. By 1922 it had recovered from the war and was ready to establish itself as the leading party of opposition. The explanation for this remarkable difference between the parties' fortunes lies partly in the context of parliamentary and cabinet politics and partly in the impact of war on the voter, as well as in long-term changes in social structure. In this way the study of the war itself sheds a clear light on some of the most important transformations in British society and politics in the twentieth century.

The chapters which follow have been grouped to be read in the order in which they are printed, though each one was written to stand on its own. The first three chapters deal with the essential issues of diplomacy and of war, 'the extension of diplomacy by other means'. David French approaches the problem of explaining grand strategy and the development of war aims by analysing the view from the centre. Britain was the pivot of the Entente, and British decisions had to allow for developments in all theatres of war, and for the conflicting and rapidly changing demands of her allies and the threats from all her enemies. The consequence of a

European civil war for Britain's global power is explored in A. J. Stockwell's study of the Empire. Bryan Ranft, inevitably, has a different perspective: the Royal Navy's problem was strategic and tactical, closely focused on the defeat of German sea-power, and his account of the naval war is therefore based on the problems of achieving victory in battle. The remaining chapters explore the impact of war on various aspects of domestic politics and society. The main contours of the war economy – men, money and munitions – are examined by Peter Dewey, while Noel Whiteside's account of the effect of an industrialized war on the civilian population indicates the range of questions which must be tackled by historians trying to evaluate the war's social benefits. Ian Beckett takes the army as a case-study of a social institution placed under great pressure by war, which contrived, surprisingly, to emerge little changed. Finally the editor's study of wartime politics explores both parliamentary politics and cabinet government under the stress of war, and the political outcome of war as seen in the 1918 general election.

1

Allies, Rivals and Enemies: British Strategy and War Aims during the First World War

DAVID FRENCH

Any historian trying to understand what the British were seeking to achieve during the First World War must be tempted at times to abandon the task in horror as he contemplates the apparently fruitless slaughter of the war. But that is the counsel of despair. The British war effort did make sense. Between 1914 and 1918 successive British governments did evolve a rational, if not always coherent, war aims programme and they did attempt to pursue it by evolving a carefully considered, if not always realistic, strategy.

The politicians and senior diplomats, soldiers and sailors who made up the British policy-making elite instinctively agreed with the German soldier and philosopher of war, Carl von Clausewitz, that war was 'a continuation of political activity by other means'.[1] They sought to secure a stable peace settlement which would safeguard the future security of Britain and her empire. In August 1914, Britain ostensibly entered the war because by invading Belgium the Germans threatened Britain's own security. Anglo-German relations had deteriorated in the years before the war because of Germany's efforts to destroy the *ententes* Britain had signed with France in 1904 and Russia in 1907, and because of her determination to build a fleet to rival the Royal Navy. These developments had convinced some policy-makers that Germany was determined to gain hegemony over Europe. But between 1912 and 1914 Anglo-German relations appeared to have improved from the low point they had reached during the Agadir crisis of 1911. Thus the sudden outbreak of war

---

1 Carl von Clausewitz, *On War*, quoted in Hew Strachan, *European Armies and the Conduct of War* (London & Boston, Mass.: Allen & Unwin, 1983), p. 94.

in August 1914 came as a shock. The British interpreted it as the result of a shift in the centre of power in Berlin. During the two preceding years, they believed, a 'peace party' bent on good relations with Britain had controlled German policy but during the July crisis they had been ousted by a 'war party' of Prussian militarists. The British therefore sought a peace settlement which would protect them from future German aggression by ending the dominance of the Prussian militarists within Germany.

At first glance this seemed a most moderate objective. But concealed beneath the apparent readiness to distinguish between militarists and the rest of the German people there lay the fact that the policy-makers could not agree upon how to achieve their aim. Politicians and the soldier-statesman Lord Kitchener, who was the Secretary of State for War between 1914 and 1916, believed that the influence of the militarists would only be eliminated after a revolution in Germany had placed power in the hands of a new and more liberal elite. But most senior soldiers shared the views of Sir Douglas Haig, the commander of the British army in France between 1916 and 1918, who told the king on 2 January 1918 that 'Few of us feel that the "democratising of Germany" is worth the loss of a single Englishman!'[2] They believed that German militarism would only be rendered impotent if Britain and her allies could inflict such a crushing military defeat on the German army that the influence of the military would be discredited for ever.

In 1914 the British realized that co-operation with France and Russia was vital if they were to prevent the Germans from winning. Their immediate objective was to lend enough support to France and Russia to prevent them from succumbing to Germany and her ally Austria-Hungary. But the British were almost as suspicious of the longer-term objectives of their friends as they were of their enemies. Most members of the policy-making elite were born between the mid-1850s and the mid-1860s and reached maturity in the late 1870s and early 1880s at a time when France and Russia were emerging as Britain's bitter colonial rivals in Africa and Asia. They had been taught to see Russian and French imperial ambitions as a danger to the security of the British Empire long before the German threat emerged. The German threat and the *ententes* of 1904 and 1907 may have muted Britain's imperial rivalries with France and Russia but they did not eliminate them. These residual suspicions were extremely influential in shaping the development of British strategy

2 *The Private Papers of Douglas Haig, 1914–1918*, ed. Robert Blake (London: Eyre & Spottiswoode, 1952), p. 277.

and war aims. Britain sought a final peace settlement which would weaken Germany but would also ensure that neither France nor more especially Russia gained so much at her expense that it in turn became a threat to the European balance of power or the security of the Empire. It would avail the British little if, in eliminating one threat, they merely built up another.

The debate within the policy-making elite during the war has been depicted as having been conducted between two sharply differing schools of thought. 'Westerners', epitomized by Haig and Sir William Robertson, the Chief of the Imperial General Staff between 1915 and 1918, were supposedly eager to commit hundreds of thousands of British troops to costly and futile battles of attrition in France and Flanders. By contrast 'Easterners' like David Lloyd George, who became Prime Minister in December 1916, and Winston Churchill, the First Lord of the Admiralty and one of the architects of the ill-fated Dardanelles campaign of 1915, were said to believe that they had found a cheaper and quicker way of defeating Germany by attacking her weaker allies, the Turks, Austrians and Bulgarians, and thus 'bringing Germany down by the process of knocking the props under her' as Lloyd George wrote on 1 January 1915.[3] But this was a caricature of reality created by the memoirs and biographies of the participants which were published in 1920s and 1930s. Books like Lloyd George's *War Memoirs*, Churchill's *The World Crisis 1911–1918* or Robertson's *Soldiers and Statesmen, 1914–1918* did not attempt to present a dispassionate history of events. They were pieces of polemical literature in which each author tried to prove that he had been right and his enemies wrong.

The real division between British policy-makers was not between 'Easterners' and 'Westerners'. It was between those like Reginald McKenna, successively Home Secretary and Chancellor of the Exchequer in the Asquith governments of 1914–16, who argued that Britain could best assist her allies by limiting the size of her own army and giving them money and equipment, and those like Robertson and Lloyd George who by the summer of 1915 championed the cause of a large conscript army as the only way of demonstrating to France and Russia that Britain had not abandoned them.

The factor which dominated British strategy between 1914 and 1918 was that she fought the war as a member of a coalition, the Entente alliance. During the war she was allied to two great powers, France and Russia, and to a series of lesser ones, including Belgium,

---

3 D. Lloyd George, *War Memoirs*, Vol. 1 (London: Odhams, 1938), p. 222.

Serbia, Japan, Italy, Romania and Greece. In April 1917 the United States of America entered the war on the side of the Entente as an Associated Power. The Entente alliance existed on four levels: military, political, naval and economic. The lesser powers, with the occasional exception of Italy, carried little weight in determining the Entente's strategy. In 1914 Britain was the strongest economic power within the Entente, but France and Russia both possessed large and powerful armies. Britain had the largest navy and it was only in the naval sphere that she dominated the Entente from the start to the finish of the war. She began the war with the smallest army of the 'big three' and did not achieve even a rough military parity with France or Russia until 1916. Initially British strategy was designed to maximize her strengths and minimize her weaknesses. The British assumed that the major burden of fighting the continental land war would fall upon France and Russia. Britain made a token contribution to the land fighting by sending the British Expeditionary Force (BEF) to northern France, but her main contribution was in the shape of the Royal Navy, which quickly blockaded the Central Powers, and the economic and financial assistance which she extended to her allies. This was the strategy of 'business as usual'. Britain became the economic powerhouse of the Entente and tried to get rich by lending her allies the money they needed to buy the weapons they required to defeat the German and Austrian armies. Meanwhile Kitchener began to raise a huge new volunteer army. He predicted that by the beginning of 1917 the French, Russian, German and Austrian armies would have exhausted their manpower reserves and fought each other to a standstill. But his New Armies would be unbloodied. Britain would be the only belligerent with large manpower reserves and she would be able to intervene, inflict a final defeat on the Central Powers and then impose her own peace terms on allies and enemies alike.

'Business as usual' promised Britain maximum victory at minimum cost. But it depended on the ability and the willingness of France and Russia to fight for two years without large-scale British military assistance. By December 1914 it was clear that this was unrealistic. Although the French and Russians thwarted the Germans' plan to achieve a quick victory in a two-front war their armies suffered horribly in doing so and by the end of 1914 the enemy was in occupation of large tracts of Allied territory. In November 1914 the Germans recognized that their only hope of winning would be to detach one of the partners from the Entente and they began to extend peace feelers to both France and Russia in the hope that they might persuade them to break with Britain. The British were alarmed when they learned of this. Before the war they knew that there had been politicians in both countries who would have preferred an understanding with Germany rather than to continue the *ententes* with Britain. In 1914–15 even those politicians friendly to Britain were aggrieved that her help was so slow in coming. A bitter joke began to circulate in Petrograd that 'the British would fight to the last Russian'.[4] In 1915–16 British strategy therefore shifted towards being seen to be doing whatever they could to give their allies material and moral assistance.

In November 1914 a further complication arose when Turkey joined the Central Powers. A small Anglo-Indian force quickly landed at Basra in Mesopotamia, ostensibly to protect the nearby oil-fields but in reality to reassert British prestige and prevent agents of the Central Powers from encouraging Muslim fundamentalists in Mesopotamia, Persia and Afghanistan from launching a holy war against British India. The Indian Mutiny of 1857 and the Mahdist rising in the Sudan in 1880s had taught the British in India and Egypt the danger which Muslim fundamentalism posed to their colonial regimes. Turkey's entry into the war also raised the question of the ultimate disposition of Constantinople. The Russians had sought to acquire the city throughout the nineteenth century to give themselves a warm-water port open to the sea. In February 1915 an Anglo-French fleet began to sail cautiously up the Dardanelles towards Constantinople. The operation was intended to knock Turkey out of the war and persuade Italy and the neutral Balkan states, Greece, Bulgaria and Romania, to join the Entente. In March it seemed to be on the point of success. Dissident Turks were conducting secret peace talks with British agents, and both the Italians and Greeks appeared eager to join the Entente. But subsequent events only highlighted the incompatibility of British and Russian policy. The Russians, fearful that Greek rather than Russian troops might liberate Constantinople and claim it for themselves, insisted that before they would agree to more states joining the Entente their allies should first promise them that Constantinople would be theirs at the end of the war. They hinted that if their wishes were not met they might seek better terms from Germany. The Greeks quickly backed away, but the British had no option but to agree to Russia's demands even though they made a negotiated peace with Turkey impossible. The Italians similarly drove a hard bargain at Austria's expense before they consented to join the Entente. Far from hasten-

4 David French, *British Strategy and War Aims, 1914–16* (London/Boston Mass.: Allen & Unwin, 1986), p. 58.

ing the end of the war, these agreements only stiffened the Central
Powers' resolve to continue fighting to prevent the dismemberment
of their own empires.

The purely naval assault at the Dardanelles had achieved nothing
by March, and therefore in April an army under Sir Ian Hamilton
landed on the Gallipoli peninsula. The failure of this landing and of
a second landing at Suvla Bay in August to silence the Turks' de-
fences encouraged Bulgaria to join the Central Powers. In October
they invaded Serbia. An Anglo-French force landed at the Greek
port of Salonika but failed to secure an escape route for the Serbian
army. By December the Germans had opened a direct railway line to
Constantinople. After weeks of indecision the British government
finally agreed to evacuate the Gallipoli peninsula before German
troops arrived in force and drove the Allied army into the sea. The
Anglo-French force remained at Salonika until the end of the war,
a source of deep distrust to many British observers. They rightly
suspected that French enthusiasm for the enterprise had much to do
with their desire to establish an informal Balkan empire after the
war. The Gallipoli débâcle at the hands of the Muslim Turks had
repercussions far beyond the peninsula. It encouraged the British in
a foolhardy attempt to save face in Muslim eyes by sending a small
force up the River Tigris to capture Baghdad. But in November the
British force was besieged at Kut and in April 1916 it was forced
into a humiliating surrender. Similarly in Egypt the British administration tried to prevent a holy war by winning over to the Entente
cause Sharif Hussein of Mecca, the guardian of the Muslim holy
cities of Mecca and Medina, by vague promises of independence
from the Turks. Later in 1915 the British and French began discussions to decide their own desiderata in the Turkish empire. These
culminated in the Sykes–Picot agreement of February 1916 which
divided Turkey in Asia into spheres of interest.

August 1915 marked a major turning point in British strategy. The
Germans drove the Russians from Poland, and occupied Warsaw
on 5 August. The Suvla Bay landing at Gallipoli failed to drive
the Turks from the peninsula, and Britain's bankers in New York
warned that they were dangerously short of funds to meet the huge
bills Britain and her allies had run up in the United States of America
to buy war supplies. Rumours that France or Russia might seek a
separate peace unless the British did more to help them intensified.
In March and May, Sir John French, the commander of the BEF,
had already mounted two assaults against the German line at Neuve
Chapelle and Festubert. They demonstrated that he did not yet have
the men, guns or shells necessary to achieve a breakthrough. But the

Allies' plight could not be ignored. On 20 August, Kitchener told his Cabinet colleagues that 'unfortunately we had to make war as we must, and not as we should like to'.[5] In late September the BEF launched the battle of Loos, not because the high command had any great hopes of securing a major military victory but because the government was afraid that if they continued their policy of withholding Britain's main effort until 1917 one or more of their major allies would desert them.

In December 1915 the military representatives of the Entente decided that the setbacks of 1915 were due to the fact that they had lacked a common plan. In 1916 they were determined to avoid this by acting in concert to mount a co-ordinated offensive in the summer of 1916 on the Western, Eastern and Italian fronts. They hoped that this would negate the Central Powers' advantage of interior lines of communication and force them to sue for peace by the end of the year. The British role in this plan was to attack north of the River Somme in co-operation with a French attack to the south of the river. The government agonized until April over whether or not to accept this recommendation. The army could only sustain such an offensive if conscription was introduced to make good the losses the BEF was likely to suffer. Some ministers, led by McKenna, were afraid that if still more men were taken from the factories and fields and placed in uniform Britain's balance of payments would collapse and she would be bankrupt before the Central Powers were beaten. But by April the majority had reluctantly agreed with Kitchener and Robertson that the war might end in an indecisive peace, or worse still a German victory, if they did not throw caution to the wind and gamble on winning the war before Britain had passed the peak of her strength.

For a few weeks in August and September 1916 it seemed as though the gamble had succeeded. The Italian offensive never really started. The French contribution on the Somme was much reduced because a large proportion of the French army was employed in defending Verdun against a German offensive which began in February. The British offensive started on 1 July and continued until November, gaining little ground at great cost but containing a large part of the German army in the west. The Russian offensive, however, was a brilliant success. Within weeks between a third and a half of the Austrian army had been killed or captured. Encouraged by this success and by the promise of an offensive by the Allied

5 G. H. Cassar, *Kitchener: Architect of Victory* (London: William Kimber, 1977), p. 389.

army at Salonika, the Romanians joined the Entente at the end of August. When the Kaiser heard this news he declared that the war was lost. By contrast some British policy-makers decided that it was time to consider detailed territorial war aims preparatory to the peace conference. The map of Europe was to be rearranged on lines broadly consistent with the principles of national self-determination. But this was tempered by a determination to re-establish a balance of power that did not leave Russia or Germany able to dominate Central and Eastern Europe and the Balkans and by the knowledge that the Entente had already promised Italy large parts of Austrian territory which were not inhabited by ethnic Italians. Germany was to lose her fleet and, if the Admiralty and the Colonial Office had their way, most of her colonies. The Admiralty feared them as bases from which Germany might again threaten Britain's imperial communications, and the Dominions and the Japanese, who had captured many of them, showed a marked reluctance throughout the war to surrender their gains.

But by December, when Lloyd George replaced Asquith as Prime Minister, hopes of an early peace had been dashed. The Germans had halted the Russian and Somme offensives and mounted a successful counter-attack in Romania which enabled them to occupy Bucharest before Christmas. Forty per cent of all the money the British spent on the war was spent in America and most of their purchases were made on credit. Only American credit and goodwill could sustain Britain and her allies into 1917 and beyond, but it was by no means certain that the Americans would give generously of either commodity. On 30 November 1916 the United States Federal Reserve Board advised American bankers to stop lending to the belligerents. On 12 December the triumphant Germans professed their readiness to discuss peace terms, and a week later the American President, Woodrow Wilson, demanded that the belligerents should announce their war aims. He hoped that this would be the first step towards a negotiated peace between equals based on democracy and justice. It would be sustained not by a return to the balance of power but by the establishment of a League of Nations. The Entente denounced the German move as a bid to divide the Allies, but they could not afford to dismiss Wilson so brusquely. Their reply to the Americans was designed to appeal to Wilson's liberal internationalism. They demanded the restoration of Serbia and Belgium, the evacuation of all occupied territory, indemnities for the damage done to them by the enemy, a new and stable regime in Europe based on the principle of nationality, guarantees of independence for small nations, the lib-

eration of the subject nationalities of the Turkish empire, and a
League of Nations to resolve future international disputes peace-
fully.

At an Allied conference held in Rome in January 1917 Lloyd
George suggested that the Allies should assist the Italians to knock
out Austria. He believed that the new Austrian Emperor, Karl, was
more ready to consider a negotiated peace than his predecessor and
hoped that a salutary defeat, which enabled the Italians to win for
themselves some of the Austrian territory the Allies had promised
them in 1915, might make him still more ready. But neither the
French, nor the Italians, nor Haig or Robertson favoured this and it
was dropped. Lloyd George then seized with enthusiasm a plan pro-
posed by the new French commander-in-chief, General Nivelle, that
if Haig's army was subordinated to him he could break through the
German line within a matter of days. Nivelle hinted that if the British
did not co-operate the French people might demand peace. Lloyd
George agreed, much to the fury of Haig and Robertson who loathed
the very idea of taking orders from a French general. The Anglo-
French offensive began successfully on 9 April when Haig's troops
captured Vimy Ridge. But Nivelle's own attacks which started on 16
April ended in a costly defeat. Nivelle was sacked and his more cautious successor, General Pétain, was determined to husband France's
fast-dwindling manpower resources. He set his face firmly against
his troops participating in any more big offensives designed to break
through the German line.

In mid-March the Tsarist government was overthrown. For some
months after the March revolution the British were unable to decide
whether or not the revolution would strengthen the Russian war effort – by removing those conservative politicians who might hanker
after a separate peace with Germany – or weaken it. The summer
provided the answer. On 18 May the new Provisional Government,
under pressure from the soviets, called on the belligerents to conclude a peace without annexations or indemnities.[6] This provoked
an enthusiastic response amongst some sections of the war-weary
labour movement in Britain. In July the Russian army launched
its final offensive, but when the Germans counter-attacked it began

6 The Provisional Government was largely composed of members of the
  various middle class liberal and left wing parties in the Duma, the Russian
  parliament. The soviets were popularly elected councils of workers and
  soldiers. For the tensions which quickly developed between these two
  groups, see L. Shapiro, *1917: The Russian Revolution and the Origins of
  Present-Day Communism* (London: Temple Smith, 1984).

rapidly to disintegrate. The Western Allies grimly concluded that Russia would probably leave the war by the end of the year.

Henceforth the British no longer had to worry about Russia as a serious imperial rival. But her defection, coupled with the fact that parts of the French army mutinied in June 1917 and that the German U-boat campaign had brought Britain to within measurable distance of starvation by the summer, meant that her military position was indeed precarious. In the summer the War Cabinet considered and rejected the possibility of a peace without victory. In the final analysis they could not tolerate the threat to British security which would persist as long as the Germans occupied the Belgian coast and there was still no indication that the Germans were ready to evacuate Belgium. Lloyd George, in response to news that the Emperor Karl might once again be ready to discuss peace terms, returned to his Italian plan. Again he was overruled. The Admiralty and Haig and Robertson preferred a British offensive in Flanders. If the Germans would not willingly evacuate Belgium, they must be expelled. Haig was confident that after one more major offensive German military manpower would be exhausted. The Admiralty was anxious to occupy the Belgian Channel ports because they believed that they were important U-boat bases.

In July the German Reichstag passed resolutions in favour of a peace of reconciliation. They were accompanied by secret talks between the German Chancellor, von Bethmann Hollweg, and the Pope, which seemed to indicate that Germany was ready to surrender Belgium. But the military high command was not and they forced the Chancellor to resign. It was some indication of just how much their military prospects had declined since January that the British did not again dismiss the possibility of a negotiated peace out of hand. In August the War Cabinet decided that a return to the *status quo ante bellum* was unacceptable but they would be willing to negotiate if the Germans would first agree to evacuate Belgium. In September the German Foreign Minister, Kuhlmann, seized on this in an attempt to separate Britain from her allies. He offered to restore to Belgium a largely fictional independence. German intermediaries also hinted to the French that they might be willing to restore Belgium, Serbia and Alsace-Lorraine and acquiesce in the loss of their own colonies if they were permitted to compensate themselves in Russia and Rumania. But the talks collapsed when Kuhlmann realized that neither France nor Britain was prepared to negotiate behind the back of her allies.

The autumn and winter of 1917 brought another series of Allied disasters. Haig's Flanders offensive, the Third Battle of Ypres, pop-

ularly known as Passchendaele, began at the end of July and when
it ended in November he was no nearer to expelling the Germans
from Belgium. In October, Italy was left prostrate after the battle
of Caporetto. The temporary euphoria aroused by the successful
tank offensive at Cambrai in November was soon deflated when the
Germans regained most of the lost ground. The only good which
came of all this was the establishment of the Supreme War Council,
an inter-Allied body to co-ordinate strategy.

In November the Bolsheviks overthrew the Russian Provisional
Government and on 15 December they signed an armistice with the
Central Powers. During the resulting peace negotiations Germany
tried to encourage war weariness amongst the Entente by falsely
claiming to support a general peace based upon the principles of
self-determination, open diplomacy and no indemnities. Trotsky, the
Bolshevik Foreign Minister, published the secret treaties of 1915–16
which threw damaging light on the Entente's imperialist war aims.
On 28 December the Labour Party insisted that it would only continue to support the war if it was certain that it was only being
fought to make the world safe for democracy and if there was an
end to secret diplomacy. Lloyd George tried to reassure them on
5 January 1918 in an address to the Trades Union Congress. He
gave only lukewarm support for France's claim to Alsace-Lorraine,
he supported Italy's claims against Austria only where they could
be justified by the principle of nationality and, in calling for the
restoration of the independence of Belgium, Serbia and Romania,
was careful not to endorse the desire of the Entente's Balkan allies
for expansion. Poland would be granted her independence, the subject races of the Austrian empire would be granted autonomy, and
Germany's colonies and the non-Turkish peoples of the Ottoman
empire would be granted a form of self-determination.

When America entered the war in April 1917, Wilson was determined to distance himself from the imperialist war aims of his
European partners. Wilson did not sign the Pact of London of
September 1914, and America did not become a formal member
of the Entente alliance. Wilson's strategy was markedly similar to
that which the British had adopted in 1914. He wanted to give the
Allies just enough assistance to defeat Germany. He assumed that
at the end of the war the Entente's governments would be politically
and economically bankrupt and he would be able to impose his own
peace plan on Allies and enemies alike. Wilson loathed 'Prussian
militarism' only slightly more than he disliked 'British navalism'.
Three days after Lloyd George spoke to the TUC, Wilson broke
his self-imposed policy of silence about America's war aims by an-

nouncing his famous Fourteen Points to Congress. These, together with the Four Principles he announced in February and the Five Particulars which he added in September, were aimed not only against Prussian militarism but against Allied imperialism as well. His calls for a European settlement based on self-determination, an impartial settlement of colonial differences, open diplomacy, free trade, and the establishment of a League of Nations could be construed in such a way as to be acceptable to the British. But his demands for freedom of the seas and a peace without indemnities or annexations clashed directly with their determination to preserve their own maritime supremacy and the Dominions' reluctance to surrender the German colonies they had captured.

By October 1917, Lloyd George had concluded that, bereft of help from her European allies and still awaiting the arrival of a powerful American army in France, Britain had no option other than to remain on the defensive in the west in 1918 and wait until 1919 before trying to deliver the final and decisive blow against Germany. If Britain mounted a singlehanded offensive in 1918, her army would be exhausted before the end of the war. The French army might have recovered and, together with the Americans, they would be able to claim the lion's share of the victory. But, with her army exhausted, Britain would be unable 'to make her voice heard and her will prevail in the momentous decisions to be come to in the Council of Peace'.[7] In the mean time he wanted the British to consolidate their position in the Middle East by knocking Turkey out of the war in 1918.

The Supreme War Council agreed to this Fabian policy, but its success depended upon the Germans obliging the Allies by remaining passive while they prepared to deliver their supreme effort. In March 1918, however, the Central Powers signed the Treaty of Brest-Litovsk with the Bolsheviks. It effectively opened Russia to further German penetration. By May their forces had occupied Sevastopol and threatened to advance into Transcaucasia, Transcaspia and perhaps even to the frontiers of India. All of Britain's gains in the Middle East, and indeed the Indian Empire itself, appeared to be threatened. On 21 March the Germany army in the west, reinforced by divisions freed by the collapse of the Russian front, began an offensive which came close to splitting the French and British armies and driving the latter into the Channel. In April 1918, Haig had to swallow his pride and agree to the French General Foch becoming

7 Harold Nicolson, *King George V: His Life and Reign* (London: Constable, 1952), p. 318.

the Allied generalissimo. It was the only way of ensuring that the French and British armies co-ordinated their operations and did not allow the Germans to defeat them singly. The Germans' initial success quickly put an end to tentative negotiations for a separate peace with Austria and Turkey which the British had been conducting in Switzerland in the winter of 1917–18. In truth they had never stood much chance of success. The Austrians had hoped they would be the first step towards a general peace negotiated by all the belligerents, but the British were only interested in achieving a separate peace with one or more of Germany's allies. In June the Entente's military situation looked so precarious that the Foreign Office was even ready to explore the implications of a speech by Kuhlmann in which he stated that the war could not be ended by military means alone. The German high command disagreed with him and forced the Kaiser to sack him.

During the summer of 1918 the British looked more than ever to Wilson for salvation, but the price he demanded was high. The Americans, who were anxious to replace sterling by the dollar as the world financial standard of value and to use American financial power to dictate Allied foreign policy, deliberately kept the British short of funds. The war had allowed American shipowners to take from the British much of the world's carrying trade. Wilson was determined that at the end of the war his country would have acquired enough merchant ships to free herself from dependence upon Britain. The British also had to pay careful attention to American political susceptibilities. It was only after lengthy negotiations that they were able to persuade Wilson to allow the Japanese to land troops at Vladivostok as part of a somewhat improbable attempt to reconstruct a military front to stop the Germans advancing beyond the Urals.

However, in mid-July the military situation in France began to improve. During the summer and autumn the Allied armies mounted a series of counter-offensives which drove the German army back beyond its start-line in March. When the collapse came it happened on all fronts. In the spring German troops had been promised that one last effort in the west would bring peace on German terms. The Allied counter-offensives deprived them of that hope, and their morale began to crumble. On 8 August the German army lost nearly 28,000 men in a single day. Two-thirds of them were prisoners. General Ludendorff, the effective commander of the army in the west, described it as 'the black day of the German army'.[8] In mid-September

8 John Terraine, *Douglas Haig: The Educated Soldier* (London: Hutchinson, 1963), p. 458.

the Allies attacked at Salonika, and by the end of the month the Bulgarians had sued for an armistice. Bulgaria's collapse opened the road to Constantinople, and the Turks quickly asked for peace. The Austrian empire disintegrated after the battle of Vittorio Veneto. This process was hastened by the promises of independence which the Allies had sown broadcast amongst the subject nationalities of the empire.

Hitherto Germany had been able to prop her allies up. Now she was no longer able to do so. On 4 October the German government appealed to Wilson for an armistice based on his Fourteen Points and his subsequent pronouncements. During the resulting negotiations the British sought armistice terms which would confirm their precarious military superiority over the Germans but which would not be so harsh as to encourage them to continue fighting. On 19 October, Haig told the War Cabinet that the German army was still not thoroughly beaten – an opinion incidentally, that was not shared by the German high command. They were equally careful not to concede too much to their friends. It was only after Wilson had accepted that any final decision on the freedom of the seas and indemnities would be reached at the peace conference, and after he had threatened to make a separate peace with the Germans, that Lloyd George agreed to accept his terms as the basis for the armistice.

By the summer of 1915, Britain's original strategy of waiting for her allies to exhaust the Central Powers before putting forth her own maximum effort was in tatters. In 1916 she gambled in an attempt to win the war before the end of the year and before her money and manpower were exhausted. A year later the European Entente powers had all but lost the war. Russia had collapsed into revolution, the French army had gone on strike, the Italians had been defeated at Caporetto and Haig's claim that German military manpower was exhausted had been shown to be wrong. It was only the promise of American dollars and men that enabled the Entente to hold on longer than the Central Powers. As the Duke of Wellington said of the battle of Waterloo, it was 'the nearest run thing you ever saw in your life'.[9]

9 R. Stewart (ed.), *The Penguin Dictionary of Political Quotations* (Harmondsworth: Penguin, 1984), p. 171.

2

The War and
the British Empire

A.J. STOCKWELL

IMPERIAL HIGH NOON?

The Great War was a clash of world empires. By 1914 overseas possessions had been transformed from the safety-valve of European tensions to the trigger of conflict between the Powers. Although Britain went to war in order to preserve the *status quo* and not to extend her global commitments, her aims diverged from this original motive as the war dragged on. From 1916 she looked forward to repartitioning the world in such a way as to prevent the resurgence of Germany in Africa, of Germany and Turkey in the Middle East and of Russia in Central Asia. In April 1917 a committee chaired by Lord Curzon drew up such a list of imperial desiderata. In the Middle East particularly, 'war imperialism' succeeded the 'informal imperialism' that had characterized British policy there before 1914.

When war broke out British imperialists were in commanding positions. Veterans of Omdurman directed the military machine; Kitchener was at the War Office and Churchill at the Admiralty. Two years later Lloyd George's reconstructed Cabinet brought to the fore a generation of unreconstructed empire-builders and 'new imperialists' of the 1890s, notably Milner, former High Commissioner in South Africa, and Curzon, former viceroy of India. These hunters were joined in 1918 by Smuts, the South African poacher turned imperial gamekeeper. Then stalked the beaters – Sykes in the Foreign Office, Amery in the Cabinet Secretariat – rousing fresh sport in Africa and Asia. In June 1918 Amery committed to paper his vision of an imperial barrier stretching west to east from the Mediterranean to the Caspian and north to south from the Arctic to the Himalayas. Reference to Smuts brings us to another feature of the Great War: the contribution of the dependencies to the Allied effort. When King George V declared war on behalf of the Empire as a whole, pledges of allegiance and aid poured in from all quarters. 'When the Empire is at war, so is Australia at war,' declared the Australian Premier, Joseph Cook. 'To the last man and the last shilling,' echoed his political opponent, A. Fisher. Similar sentiment came forth from New Zealand and Canada, and even South Africa assisted Britain despite 'armed protest' in December 1914 and the resurgence of Afrikaner nationalism led by Hertzog. At Westminster, Redmond committed his Irish party to the British cause. In India politicians and princes expressed profusions of fealty in resolutions and rupees.

Two and a half million men from the Empire beyond the British Isles fought in the war. Nearly 1½ million of these were Indian volunteers. They were supported by thousands of non-combatants like the 82,000 Egyptians and 92,000 Chinese serving in labour units in November 1918. A relatively high percentage of the white male populations of the Dominions served overseas in the armed forces: 19.35 per cent from New Zealand, 13.48 per cent from Canada, 13.43 per cent from Australia and 11.12 per cent from South Africa compared with Britain's 22.11 per cent. Over 62,000 Indians died in battle, while Australia's fatalities were more than the number suffered by the United States, whose population was twenty times larger.[1] India paid most of the costs incurred by her troops while serving outside the subcontinent with the result that India's military expenditure rose from £20 million in 1913–14 to £140 million in 1918–19. In 1916 she took over £100 million of the British government's war loan, a gift which was equivalent to a year's revenue for the Government of India. Canada, Australia and New Zealand bore the total cost of their forces, and South Africa paid for the South-West African campaign and much of the maintenance of its troops in the East African theatre.[2] In addition, and in spite of the dislocation of world trade, many calls were made on the imperial producers of commodities vital to the war effort.

Furthermore, it can be argued that overseas dependencies played a crucial role in military strategy. Initially swift attacks were launched

1 Estimates of manpower vary. The figures here are from *Statistics of the Military Effort of the British Empire in the Great War* (London: War Office, 1922) and have been summarized by C. E. Carrington, 'The Empire at war, 1914–1918', in *The Cambridge History of the British Empire (CHBE)*, Vol. 3 (Cambridge: Cambridge University Press, 1959), pp. 641–2.

2 Expenditure specifically on the war effort is not easily itemized and estimates vary: ibid., pp. 642–3.

Map 2.1: The War in Africa, 1914–18

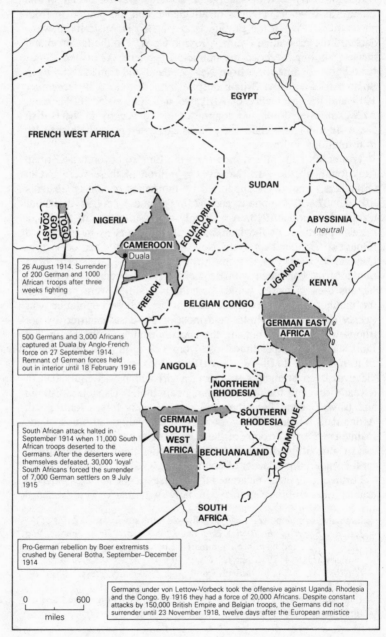

EGYPT

FRENCH WEST AFRICA

SUDAN

ABYSSINIA
(neutral)

TOGO
GOLD COAST

NIGERIA

CAMEROON
Duala

EQUATORIAL AFRICA

FRENCH

UGANDA

KENYA

BELGIAN CONGO

GERMAN EAST AFRICA

26 August 1914. Surrender of 200 German and 1000 African troops after three weeks fighting

500 Germans and 3,000 Africans captured at Duala by Anglo-French force on 27 September 1914. Remnant of German forces held out in interior until 18 February 1916

ANGOLA

NORTHERN RHODESIA

SOUTHERN RHODESIA

MOZAMBIQUE

South African attack halted in September 1914 when 11,000 South African troops deserted to the Germans. After the deserters were themselves defeated, 30,000 'loyal' South Africans forced the surrender of 7,000 German settlers on 9 July 1915

GERMAN SOUTH-WEST AFRICA

BECHUANALAND

SOUTH AFRICA

Pro-German rebellion by Boer extremists crushed by General Botha, September–December 1914

0　　　　600

miles

Germans under von Lettow-Vorbeck took the offensive against Uganda, Rhodesia and the Congo. By 1916 they had a force of 20,000 Africans. Despite constant attacks by 150,000 British Empire and Belgian troops, the Germans did not surrender until 23 November 1918, twelve days after the European armistice on German coaling and cable stations to knock out the enemy's global network of communications, to secure for the Royal Navy the freedom of the seas and to facilitate an economic blockade of the Central Powers. The very first engagement of the war occurred when a small force from the British colony of the Gold Coast occupied the German cable station in Togoland (West Africa). Meanwhile the navy scoured the seas and destroyed a German force under von Spee off the Falklands in December 1914. Other attacks upon German colonies developed into more prolonged operations in the Cameroons, German East and South-West Africa (Map 2.1), as well as in German New Guinea and German Samoa.

Successes overseas encouraged those in London who were dismayed by the gathering stalemate on the Western Front to urge the adoption of an 'Eastern Front' which, they argued, would allow mobility, take the pressure off the Russian allies, turn the flank of the Central Powers and strike at the enemy's 'soft underbelly'. From November 1914 onwards the war against the Ottoman Turks provided such an opportunity. Egypt, that imperial anvil upon which had been hammered out Britain's imperial strategy since the Napoleonic wars, now became the fulcrum of the 'Eastern Front'. The Gallipoli campaign of 1915 was part of this; Mesopotamia (Iraq) was another 'Eastern' venture. Both were disasters: in the one, Australia and New Zealand played heroic parts and suffered huge losses with the result that 25 April has been honoured ever since in those countries as ANZAC Day; in the other, some 3,000 British and 6,000 Indian troops were led into captivity when General Townshend surrendered at Kut in April the following year. These defeats were followed by victories: T. E. Lawrence stirred the Arab revolt; in March 1917 Baghdad was captured and in December of that year Allenby marched into Jerusalem. One by one Turkey's Arab dominoes were tumbling and Britain was acquiring a portfolio of enormous and sometimes conflicting obligations in the Middle East. When the war with Turkey ended on 30 October 1918 Britain was supreme throughout the Islamic world (Map 2.2).

Yet, however dramatic the gains and losses in the extra-European regions, it was in Flanders that the Great War was to be decided. Here, too, imperial troops played a part: ten divisions of infantry from Canada, Australia and New Zealand, and two divisions of Indian cavalry were shipped in. The Canadians have particularly poignant memories of Ypres and Arras; over 11,000 Canadians were lost in the taking of Vimy Ridge in April 1917.

Service in a common cause consolidated the organization of em-

Map 2.2: The Collapse of the Ottoman Empire, 1912–23

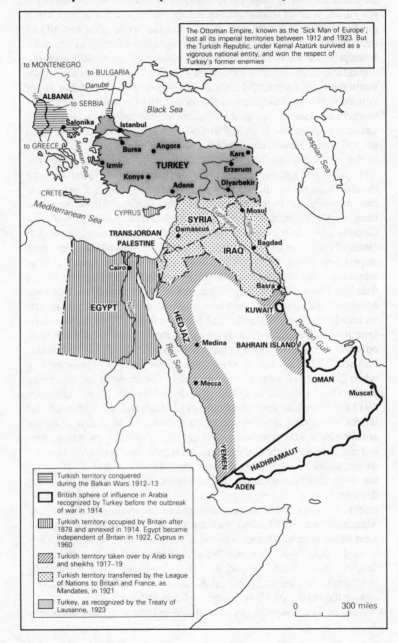

The Ottoman Empire, known as the 'Sick Man of Europe', lost all its imperial territories between 1912 and 1923. But the Turkish Republic, under Kemal Atatürk survived as a vigorous national entity, and won the respect of Turkey's former enemies

to MONTENEGRO
to BULGARIA
Danube
ALBANIA
to SERBIA
Salonika
Istanbul
Black Sea
to GREECE
Bursa
Angora
Kars
Aegean Sea
Izmir
TURKEY
Erzerum
Konya
Adana
Diyarbekir
Caspian Sea
CRETE
Mediterranean Sea
CYPRUS
Mosul
SYRIA
Damascus
Euphrates
Tigris
TRANSJORDAN
PALESTINE
IRAQ
Bagdad
Cairo
Basra
EGYPT
KUWAIT
Nile
HEDJAZ
Red Sea
Medina
BAHRAIN ISLAND
Persian Gulf
Mecca
OMAN
Muscat
YEMEN
HADHRAMAUT
ADEN

Turkish territory conquered during the Balkan Wars 1912–13

British sphere of influence in Arabia recognized by Turkey before the outbreak of war in 1914

Turkish territory occupied by Britain after 1878 and annexed in 1914. Egypt became independent of Britain in 1922, Cyprus in 1960

Turkish territory taken over by Arab kings and sheikhs 1917–19

Turkish territory transferred by the League of Nations to Britain and France, as Mandates, in 1921

Turkey, as recognized by the Treaty of Lausanne, 1923

0   300 miles

pire. During Kitchener's period as Secretary of State for War, military instructions emanated from London with scant attention being paid to the views of the Dominions. Increased centralism also appeared in the mobilization of resources and economic planning. Following the economic conference of the Allies in Paris in June 1916, a committee chaired by Lord Balfour of Burleigh considered British commercial and industrial policy for the postwar period. As it examined ways of safeguarding domestic industries, recovering lost markets and developing Empire resources, the emphasis shifted first from Allied unity against the enemy to imperial protection against the foreigner, and later from the well-being of the Empire as a whole to the pursuit of national self-interest. The final report, submitted in 1918, was 'a document of Great Britain's national economic policy' in which 'Allied solidarity was almost entirely forgotten and imperial questions were surveyed perfunctorily at second hand'.[3] At the same time pressure groups like the Empire Resources Development Committee advocated the more systematic exploitation of colonial estates for Britain's benefit. The most remarkable moves towards imperial integration came at the highest level in December 1916 when Lloyd George set up the Imperial War Cabinet comprising the five War Cabinet members plus further British and Dominion ministers. In the strict sense of the term this was no Cabinet at all since its members were answerable to their several parliaments. None the less, it discussed major issues of war and peace and marked a major advance in imperial consultation as compared with the situation that had obtained in 1911, at the last Imperial Conference before the war, when Sir Edward Grey had merely informed Dominion leaders of the foreign policy of His Majesty's Government. In the spring of 1917 the Imperial War Cabinet met fourteen times in the space of six weeks to consider strategy and in the summer of 1918 it reconvened with the prospect of planning the peace settlement.

Four great empires – Habsburg, Hohenzollern, Ottoman, Romanov – collapsed under the strain of world war. Yet the British Empire survived and even expanded. On 1 November 1918, Great Britain deployed the largest army and navy in her history. Territorially her empire was at its fullest extent; new territory (later to be known as Mandates under the League of Nations) had been occupied in West, East and Southern Africa, in the Pacific and in the Middle East.[4] For

3 W. K. Hancock, *Survey of British Commonwealth Affairs*, Vol. 2, Pt I, *Problems of Economic Policy 1918-1939* (London: Oxford University Press for the Royal Institute of International Affairs, 1940), pp. 97–8.
4 Mandates received by the British Empire were as follows: to Austra-

a time, indeed, the British Empire stretched in an unbroken swath from Suez to Singapore. The dreams of Curzon and Amery had been fulfilled. Imperial integrity surely demonstrated the right of Britain's cause in war; victory on the battlefield was taken to authenticate Britain's imperial record. Bloodshed in 1914–18 had been an imperial sacrament. A month after the armistice the commander in chief in India wrote: 'Now that it is all over and the Empire stands on a pinnacle built by her tenacity and courage – never did our reputation stand as high.'[5] It was to all appearances the imperial high noon; perhaps 1918 not 1940 was the Empire's finest hour. Empire had contributed to victory; victory had enhanced empire.

IMPERIAL SUNSET?

Yet this is a questionable equation. Just how significant was the overseas empire's contribution to Allied victory? Just how beneficial to imperial cohesion were the costs and the spoils of victory? Although every instance of colonial assistance in the war effort made for good propaganda, behind the scenes Whitehall complained that the Dominions and India were not pulling their weight; some went so far as to claim that they required as much support as they provided. In military terms, after all, the imperial theatres of the Middle East, Africa and the Pacific remained 'side-shows' to the main conflict on the Western Front. Moreover, these 'side-shows' can be regarded as wasteful distractions from, rather than useful contributions to, the major effort: they diverted men and materials away from Europe and into the defence of possessions that hinged upon the Indian Raj. In other words, imperial commitments dispersed and prolonged the endeavours. The figures of military deployment on 1 November 1918 are instructive on this point. A total of 101 British and imperial divisions were disposed on various fronts of which seventy-one were British and the other thirty originated in the Dominions and in India (Table 2.1). The 30 per cent contribution from the dependencies was no mean proportion but further examination reveals that of the 64 Divisions in France, the crux of the conflict,

lia, German possessions in the Pacific south of the Equator; to New Zealand, German Samoa; to South Africa, German South-West Africa; to the United Kingdom, Palestine, Iraq, German East Africa (Tanganyika), portions of the Cameroons and Togoland. See K.C. Wheare, 'The Empire and the peace treaties, 1918–1921', *CHBE*, Vol. 3, pp. 657-8.

5 Sir Charles Monro to Sir Henry Rawlinson, 12 December 1918, quoted by Keith Jeffery, *The British Army and the Crisis of Empire 1918–22* (Manchester: Manchester University Press, 1984), p. 1.

only ten were imperial as distinct from British. The prime function of imperial contingents was, therefore, not to win the European war but to defend and, if need be, to add to the overseas empire. Indeed, the Indian Corps, dispatched to France in 1914-15, failed to adjust to the novelties of industrialized and bureaucratized warfare being fought on the Western Front.

Table 2.1   *Deployment of British and Imperial fighting formations on the various fronts at 1 November 1918*

	British		Dominion		Indian		
Divisions	*Cavalry*	*Infantry*	*Cav.*	*Inf.*	*Cav.*	*Inf.*	*Total*
France	3	51	–	10	–	–	64
Italy	–	3	–	–	–	–	3
Palestine	–	1	2	–	2	6	11
Salonika	–	4	–	–	–	–	4
Mesopotamia	–	1	–	–	1	4	6
India	–	3	–	–	–	3	6
E. Africa	–	–	–	–	–	–	2*
UK	1	4	–	–	–	–	5
Total	4	67	2	10	3	13	101

* A mixed force of British, white South African and African troops.
Source: *Statistics of the Military Effort of the British Empire in the Great War* (London: War Office, 1922), summarized by C. E. Carrington, 'The Empire at War, 1914-1918', *Cambridge History of the British Empire*, Vol. 3 (Cambridge: Cambridge University Press, 1959), p. 641.

After the Armistice manpower shortages did not cease to vex the military, for Lloyd George, under pressure to bring the boys back to 'a fit country for heroes to live in', embarked upon rapid demobilization. By the middle of 1919 Britain's army of 5 million had shrunk to 1 million; at the end of the year the War Office was hard put to it to raise a single infantry division in Britain for any emergency that was likely to arise from Ireland to Iraq. Consequently, on the outbreak of peace the British government came to rely, even more perhaps than during the war itself, upon the co-operation of the Dominions and the direct utilization of the human and material resources of dependencies, notably those of India, for maintaining the Paris settlement and protecting recent conquests. India was still the imperial fire-brigade which in the nineteenth century had quenched bushfires of colonial resistance on the fringes of the Indian Ocean and kept the Russians at bay in the Asian 'Great Game'.

Domestic considerations – democracy and demobilization, industrial unrest and financial indebtedness, retrenchment in expenditure and economic rehabilitation – tempted statesmen to call in the Empire to redress weakness at home and reassert authority in a world where former international arrangements no longer applied. If the imperial role during the war had amounted to little more than a side-show, then empire stood centre-stage in policing the peace.

This brings us to the second question raised at the start of this section: What impact did the First World War have upon imperial fraternity? As early as March 1915, Milner, looking forward to peace and ruminating upon the effects of the Seven Years War of 1756–63 (the war that provoked Anglo-American conflict and the eventual loss of the thirteen colonies), warned his countrymen: 'Remember that on a previous and most disastrous occasion it was not war – not the strain of war – which disrupted the Empire, but the aftermath of war. This is a risk which we ought not to run....'[6] The British Empire was never more than a hotchpotch of Dominions, Crown Colonies, Protectorates, Princely States and so forth. Each category was in a different constitutional relationship with Britain; the whole was marked by political decentralization and *laissez-faire* economics. Structurally deficient and without natural coherence, the British Empire, it seemed to some, was tottering towards disintegration; the vigour of 1914–18 amounted to death throes, the imperial fervour merely its obsequies. A country that had sacrificed the flower of its youth lacked not just the will, it had lost the means to keep an empire. As Britain strove to sustain global power, so she dug deep into the pockets of subject peoples. The more she tapped these resources, the greater the danger of resistance to the imperial connection.

In December 1919 the Viceroy of India protested about the cost, borne by India, of maintaining 180,000 Indian troops on imperial business throughout the Middle East:

> I must point out also that India in this way is being exploited by the War Office because they find that they can maintain Indian troops abroad without those extremely objectionable questions in Parliament which would be asked if they were British and not Indian forces.[7]

6 Quoted in W. K. Hancock, *Survey of British Commonwealth Affairs*, Vol. 1, *Problems of Nationality, 1918–1936* (London: Oxford University Press for the Royal Institute of International Affairs, 1937), p. 65.

7 Chelmsford to Montagu, 19 December 1919, quoted by Jeffery, *British*

Eighteen months later, in June 1921 the Indian government was grappling with its own vast problems, including Gandhi's civil disobedience campaign, and it bluntly warned London of the dangers of imperial over-rule: 'Public opinion in India will not tolerate any longer a system under which our [Indian] troops are [used]...to suit the fluctuating requirements of His Majesty's Government.'[8] General Rawlinson diagnosed the essential cause of the problem as public financial constraint. He wrote in January 1922:

> The fact of the matter is that the cost of the British soldier has gone up so inordinately since the war that no country [i.e. neither Britain nor India] can afford to maintain him. As a result, it is difficult to see how we can keep this Empire together.[9]

Geddes axed expenditure at home; Inchcape chaired a committee on Indian retrenchment; the Federation of British Industry exhorted the government to thrift in Crown Colony spending too. If India's reliability as the empire's policeman was in doubt, so too was the internal security of the Raj itself. British manpower in the subcontinent after the outbreak of the First World War, when it amounted to 75,000, had declined markedly; at one point during the war the number of British troops in India (as distinct from the Indian Army) dropped to 15,000, that is to say some 23,000 fewer than there had been on the eve of the Indian Mutiny in 1857.

It was not only soldiers that were expensive and in short supply. At the Washington Conference, 1921–2, Britain agreed to limit the production of capital ships to the ratio of five British to five American to three Japanese, thus spelling out in the clearest terms the end of naval hegemony upon which the nineteenth century empire had rested. Administrators also were thin on the ground. During the war there was a flight of officials from the colonies to the colours with the result that government services in India and the tropics were severely depleted. In the Gold Coast, for example, 613 Europeans were employed in civil administration at the start of the war; by late 1917 this figure had dropped by 15 per cent to 521, and of these a further ninety were on secondment to the Gold Coast Regiment serving outside the colony or in the occupied territory of Togoland, thereby reducing the complement of Gold Coast administrators to approximately 430.[10] As numbers dwindled, those left behind worked

Army, p. 53.
8 Viceroy to Secretary of State, 6 June 1921, quoted in ibid., p. 58.
9 Rawlinson to Sir H. Wilson, 4 January 1922, quoted in ibid., p. 59.
10 See *Gold Coast Annual Report, 1914*, et seqq.

longer hours, surrendered home leave and experienced straitened living conditions as a result of wartime inflation. Feeling frustrated and forgotten in a backwater, they occasionally overreacted to outbursts of local resistance as, for example, occurred in Bongo (Northern Territories) where a rising that followed the withdrawal of a company of the Gold Coast Regiment was ferociously suppressed with the loss of fifty-nine lives, the destruction of compounds and the seizure of livestock. Raising the morale of the colonial service had not been easy for the wartime governor, who had himself lost his only son and a brother on the Western Front. 'We have seen some heavy years – you and I,' he reminded the public service as he prepared to leave the colony in 1919.

> During that time I have often thought of us here in the Gold Coast as resembling the galley-slaves of old – bound and chained to the rowing-bench, tugging doggedly at our sweeps, and listening in the darkness of the orlop, in an agony of uncertainty and suspense, to the stamping feet of the fighting-men on the deck planks overhead.... [11]

To return to India; it was after the Great War that the composition of the Indian Civil Service began to change significantly with a greater proportion of Indian recruits joining the ranks of the 'heaven born' every year.

War sapped the Empire, and cracks opened up on the surface. Military sacrifices and conscription of 'native labour', the accumulation of mountains of unexported agricultural surpluses in the tropics and the emergence of import substitute industries elsewhere, a growing awareness of British fallibility and the propagation of both Bolshevik ideology and American anti-imperialism, all encouraged centrifugal tendencies in the imperial conglomerate. Britain's war with the Ottoman Caliph, the leader of Islam, caused unrest amongst her Muslim subjects. In 1915 an Indian regiment stationed in Singapore mutinied; for a time the whole colony was threatened and, when control was restored, the punishments meted out to mutineers were draconian, forty-seven of them being sentenced to death. From December 1915 to the following April the Sheikh of Senussi launched a *jihad* against the British in the western desert, and in April 1916 an expedition was mounted against Ali Dinnar of Darfur in the Sudan. The latter was, incidentally, the last occasion when British troops were drawn up in the famous red-square formation characteristic of

11 Sir Hugh Clifford, speech at a dinner of the Gold Coast Public Service, Accra, 26 March 1919, in Clifford Papers in the possession of Mr. H.C. Holmes.

nineteenth-century frontier wars. At Easter 1916 came the Dublin rising which sparked a train of events culminating in the Anglo-Irish Treaty of 1921, the partition of Ireland and the entry of the Irish Free State into the Commonwealth on the same footing as Canada. Wartime campaigning for Indian home rule and the Lucknow Pact of 1916 between Congress and the Muslim League convinced the Viceroy and the Liberal Secretary of State of the need for a political initiative with the result that Edwin Montagu on 20 August 1917 declared in Parliament that Britain's goal in India was the 'progressive realization of responsible government'. They followed this up in 1919 with a package of constitutional reforms granting a large measure of self-government to the Indian provinces. Rocked within by riot and revolt, the Empire faced the prowling hosts of Midian on the borders with Afghanistan, southern Russia, Mesopotamia and Somaliland.

The self-governing Dominions of British kith and kin were also asserting themselves more obtrusively. The most loyal of them all had been 'Australianized' by the Gallipoli experience and the ANZAC legend fostered by C. E. W. Bean in his official history of the Australian Imperial Force.[12] In 1917–18 the three principal premiers (Borden of Canada, Hughes of Australia and Smuts of South Africa) were looking forward to recasting their relationship with London so as to give 'full recognition of the Dominions as autonomous nations of an Imperial Commonwealth' with the right to 'an adequate voice in foreign policy' by means of 'continuous consultation' and 'concerted action'.[13] They also insisted on separate representation at the Paris Peace Conference. Practical considerations and, in the case of Australia and South Africa, the prospect of the indefinite enjoyment of territorial conquests in the Pacific and South West Africa outweighed constitutional theory in their eagerness not to leave the settlement to the Big Three. Were war and its aftermath to be, as Milner had feared, the solvent of empire? When Lloyd George called upon the Dominions to join Britain in upholding the Treaty of Sèvres at the time of the Chanak crisis in 1922, the Prime Minister of Canada, Mackenzie King, resented what he took to be London's patronizing assumption that the Dominions would

12 *The Official History of Australia in the War of 1914-1918*, 12 Vols. (Sydney: Angus & Robertson, 1921-37), of which C. E. W. Bean edited four volumes on the war in France and two on the Dardanelles campaign.

13 *Report of the Imperial War Conference, 1917*, Resolution IX, in R. M. Dawson, ed., *The Development of Dominion Status 1900–1936* (London: Oxford University Press, 1937), p. 175.

agree more or less automatically to support British-led operations
in Asia Minor and insisted that it was for the Canadian Parliament
'to decide whether or not we should participate in wars in different
parts of the world'.[14] Perhaps the years 1916–22 mark the sunset
rather than the high noon of empire.

RETURN TO NORMALCY?

After the Great War British governments could afford neither to surrender nor to rule the Empire. Their quandary lay at the heart of
the imperial crisis of 1918–22. Britain needed the economic and
strategic benefits of empire as never before, yet the demands she
made of empire loosened its linkages. The clear-headed might argue that logic pointed to the abandonment of the indefensible and
the exploitation of the weak. In the confusion that so often passed
for policy there was a bit of both attitudes; for example, Britain
pulled out of Persia yet General Dyer slaughtered demonstrators at
Amritsar. However, neither approach dominated the official mind
of British imperialism after 1918. Policy-makers were in no mood
to retreat from empire nor, for that matter, did they relish shoulder-
ing its burdens. Side by side with the patriotism of Greater Britain
lay the hard-headedness of Little England.   Direct colonial rule
with all its costs and complications had been accepted by London in
the previous century almost always with reluctance. Power without
obligations had been the preferred option. Imperial strategy after the
Great War, like so many aspects of British public life, reverted to
normalcy as government set about maximizing the benefits of overseas bases, markets and investments, and minimizing its involve-
ment in irksome local difficulties on the periphery. Interest revived
in tariff reform, imperial preference and colonial development as
means to solving the economic problems of the mother country, and
there was a fresh commitment (through, for example, the creation
of the Mandate of Palestine and Trans-Jordan) to the security of
the eastern Mediterranean and the route to India. At the same time
British governments tried to shed the more extravagant territorial
responsibilities acquired during the Great War.   British objectives
remained nineteenth-century objectives, although they were pursued
in starkly different circumstances.

After the First World War, Britain employed a variety of techniques to bridge the gulf between her far-flung global interests and

14 W. L. Mackenzie King, Canadian House of Commons, 1 February 1923,
    quoted in Dawson *Development of Dominion Status*, pp. 239 ff.

her reduced capacity. They can be examined under four heads though they are all aspects of the evolving and essentially collaborative relationship between elites within the Empire. The first was the course of diplomacy and consisted of the careful cajoling of Britain's self-governing Commonwealth partners to win general support for Britain's direction of the Commonwealth alliance. Following the Imperial Conference of 1921, the first to be convened since the conclusion of hostilities, Lloyd George explained to the House of Commons the nature of the postwar imperial relationship which, he said, enabled strength through unity and unity through partnership.

> The sole control of Britain over foreign policy is now vested in the Empire as a whole. That is a new fact .... The advantage to us is that joint control means joint responsibility, and when the burden of Empire has become so vast it is well that we should have the shoulders of these young giants under the burden to help us along. It introduces a broader and calmer view into foreign policy. It restrains rash Ministers, and it will stimulate timorous ones.[15]

Not that it restrained Lloyd George the following year from rashly presuming upon the unquestioning support of the Dominions during the Chanak crisis. Australia complained of inadequate consultation; Canada argued in favour of 'plural foreign policies' for Dominions according to their respective interests and regional spheres. Chanak contributed to the downfall of Lloyd George's coalition government and it renewed the debate within the Commonwealth about the nature of Dominion status which was defined upon the principle of equality in 1926. This definition and its legalization in the 1931 Statute of Westminster added to the complications of maintaining the Commonwealth alliance.

The second technique was the creation and reinforcement of client states and was particularly favoured in that area of the Middle East which had been under the Ottoman Turks.[16] Iraq was an amenable client, but Iran was not. In order to win local compliance and at the same time eliminate indigenous interference in wider imperial matters, Britain was prepared to make apparently generous concessions in the field of local administration. This was the third of the four imperial techniques and was practised, for example, in Egypt where the British negotiated an agreement with Zaghlul Pasha and the na-

---

15 Lloyd George, speaking in the House of Commons, 14 December 1921, quoted in Dawson, *Development of Dominion Status*, p. 211.
16 See J. G. Darwin, *Britain, Egypt and the Middle East: Imperial Policy in the Aftermath of War, 1918-1922* (London: Macmillan, 1981).

tionalists, and in India where the postwar Montagu–Chelmsford reforms created provincial diarchy (or partial responsible government).
The fourth technique of collaboration was more administrative than
political; by means of 'indirect rule', which was given some theo-
retical and practical coherence in the writings of Frederick Lugard,
Britain delegated tasks like the collection of revenue or policing to
the traditional authorities of tribal societies. Indirect rule was an
age-old response to a frontier situation but in the 1920s it became a
sacrosanct principle of 'native administration' in British Africa.

In addition to these diplomatic, political, constitutional and administrative devices, the British still called upon the military for
holding the Empire together.[17] The emphasis now switched to mobility and, so far as was possible, the infantry was replaced by the
tactical strike force as in, for example, the use of air power against
Iraqi rebels in the 1920s. Similarly, the Royal Navy still patrolled
the sea-lanes, displaying power in the hope that such display would
obviate the necessity of backing up the appearance with the actu-
ality of power. Imperialism after the war was, as ever, a gigantic
confidence trick and the British made the fullest use of great or-
namental occasions like the Prince of Wales's tours and the 1935
jubilee, imperial conferences in London and durbars in New Delhi,
and the Empire Exhibition at Wembley in 1924. The shrewdest men
of power compensated for the limitations of their power by bluff;
the gauche and heavy-handed paraded their weakness by bluster.

Pomp and partnership, consultation and conciliation: such were
the ploys of postwar imperialism. Yet the more Britain made concessions in what were regarded as inessentials, the more exposed
became the essentials of the imperial relationship and the more tenuous London's determining influence. It has been argued by some
that the Dominions' achievement of autonomy and neutrality in foreign affairs inhibited a vigorous British stand against the European
dictators in the 1930s. Similarly, as Indians asserted themselves in
provincial government and closed their grip upon the purse strings
of local administration, so the dependability of India as the 'barrack-
room of empire' was called into question. Again, as British-policy
in Palestine snagged on conflicting obligations to Arab and Jew dat-
ing from the Balfour Declaration of 1917, so imperial strength in the
eastern Mediterranean was jeopardized. During the Great War, the
Zionist Chaim Weizmann had argued that 'a reconstructed Palestine
will become a very great asset to the British empire', yet so in-

17 See Jeffery, *British Army*, and Anthony Clayton, *The British Empire as
    a Superpower, 1919–39* (London: Macmillan, 1986).

tractable was the Palestinian problem becoming in the 1930s that Britain was in no position to exploit the strategic advantages of the Mandate when Mussolini invaded Abyssinia. Finally, the bluff of imperial defence was called when the Japanese invaded South-East Asia in December 1941. The *Repulse* and *Prince of Wales* were sent to the bottom of the South China Sea and the 'impregnable' naval base of Singapore surrendered, thereby revealing to all the world what service chiefs had been striving to conceal since the early 1920s: British inability to protect a two-hemisphere empire.

The Great War did not categorically signal the beginning of the end of the British Empire. As we have seen, there was considerable continuity in attitudes and policies between the prewar and postwar periods; indeed, in many respects, the war resulted in the expansion and consolidation of empire and in renewed enthusiasm on the part of the British government for holding fast to its economic and strategic benefits. While clubland blimps nostalgically revered the eminent empire-builders whom the Bloomsbury Group held up to ridicule, Whitehall mandarins were more pragmatic than either when it came to the pursuit of the national interest. Officials made adjustments in Britain's relations with Dominion governments, Indian politicians and leadership elites in the colonies with the intention of promoting British influence. They did not plan the demission of power or even anticipate the storms ahead; neither did they see themselves as running before the wind and meekly 'selling the pass'. On the contrary, even in the aftermath of the Second World War the British Empire would still be a force, the 'third force', in world affairs. However, as has been the experience of other empires, metropolitan Britain grew increasingly dependent upon what had once been its dependencies and these it was less and less capable of either controlling or conciliating.

Given that world power begins at home, historians would be advised to seek the explanation for these imperial difficulties in the decline of the first industrial nation, if not the death of liberal England, rather than focus upon the emergence of colonial nationalist movements. After the First World War the British government faced a tripled electorate, rampant trade unions, an enormous national debt and continuing rebellion in Ireland. There was no question of it further hazarding domestic peace end prosperity by calling upon the nation to spring to the defence of the Empire. After four years of world war, attention swung to problems on the home front. Nevertheless, there was also no question of the British establishment abandoning the world authority for which that war had been fought. If Britain could not afford to run the Empire, she hoped that others might be induced to do it at her behest. This was an old stratagem – British India had been footing the bill for a century and a half already – but the postwar demands made by a weakened metropole were more intensive and more intrusive than ever before. Ultimately they would be more resistible, too.

3

The Royal Navy
and the War at Sea

BRYAN RANFT

INTRODUCTION

For the Royal Navy the war was full of paradox and disappointment. The Grand Fleet, whose superiority in capital ships was the outcome of the naval race with Germany, failed to gain the decisive victory confidently expected of it. In the one full fleet action, at Jutland on 31 May 1916, its losses in ships and men considerably exceeded those of the German High Seas Fleet. It spent the rest of the war frustrated by inability to bring the enemy to action again, and its existence seemed irrelevant to the defeat of Germany's nearly successful attempt to conquer Britain by its submarine campaign against merchant shipping. When this campaign was finally checked in 1917 it was by the institution of convoy, a method of protection which had been condemned as useless by the great bulk of naval opinion since the 1880s. Yet there was victory at sea. In November 1918 the German fleet steamed into internment, and subsequent scuttling, at Scapa Flow, surrounded by a Grand Fleet of increased superiority and hitting power and whose morale and fighting spirit were in complete contrast to the disillusioned and mutinous German crews. The defeat of the submarine campaign, unnecessarily late though it was in coming, had saved the country from starvation and industrial collapse. In Germany, on the other hand, the effectiveness of the naval blockade in cutting off virtually all seaborne trade and supplies, had contributed significantly to the political and military collapse of the Wilhelmine empire. The navy had not won the war – that was done in France and Flanders – but, without victory at sea, the land battle could never have been sustained.

Whatever the final success, the path to it was littered with frustrations and failures, much to the disappointment of popular opinion

which had confidently expected that the upstart German navy would
be rapidly defeated in battle by a Royal Navy with superior numbers
and a fighting spirit based on centuries of naval supremacy. This
belief was reinforced by a general acceptance of the ideas of the
most widely read naval theorist of the day, the American Admiral
A. T. Mahan, who had proclaimed that victory at sea would always
be gained by the superior battle fleet which would win command
of the sea: the ability to use the seas for strategic and economic
purposes and to deny that command to the enemy.[1] Translating this
into British terms, what was expected was another Trafalgar which
would virtually end the war at sea. That Trafalgar itself had not
accomplished this tended to be forgotten by both naval and popular
opinion.

What actually happened in 1914–18 was very different. Why
were the expectations of quick victory unfulfilled? Was it entirely
because of the incompetence of the British naval high command, as
judgements made by politicians near the time and by later historians
have strongly claimed? Or were there factors in the strategic situation and in the make-up of navies and in the particular problems of
war at sea which made the prophecies of a quick decision impossible
to realize? A balanced examination of the evidence shows that the
latter is the truer explanation.

TECHNOLOGICAL CHANGE

Central to this interpretation is an appreciation of the impact of
technological change on naval warfare. An illuminating general-
ization, although subject to detailed reservations, is that if a naval
commander or seaman had been transported in time from Drake's
encounter with the Spanish Armada in 1588 to Nelson's 1805 victory
at Trafalgar he would have found the tasks of manoeuvring the fleet
and using his weapons completely familiar. Similarly moved from
Trafalgar to Jutland, he would have been completely bewildered.
Everything had changed, the battleships much bigger and made of
steel instead of wood, driven by steam instead of sail at unheard-of
speeds and armed with guns and shells capable of destroying their
opponents at ranges measured in thousands of yards compared with
the hundreds of yards of smooth bore cannon. At Trafalgar the opposing fleets had come into action at a combined speed of under 4

1 A. T. Mahan, *Naval Strategy* (London: Sampson Low, 1911); D. M.
   Schurman, *The Education of a Navy: The Development of British Naval
   Strategic Thought, 1867–1914* (London: Cassell, 1965), pp. 60–82, is a
   good analysis of Mahan's ideas and significance.

knots; at Jutland they approached each other at over 40 knots. The main gun engagements at Trafalgar were fought at 200 yards; at Jutland the main capital-ship actions were at ranges of up to 16,000 yards. Neither of the commanders-in-chief at Jutland had had any previous experience on which to base his strategic decisions, nor had the battleships' captains and crews any experience of fighting their ships and weapons. There had been the Russo-Japanese war of 1904–5 but the sides had been so unevenly matched that no clear lessons could be learned. It was not only capital ships and their guns which had been transformed. New weapons in the shape of mines and torpedoes had emerged. The Japanese war had shown that the destructive power of underwater explosions, even against the most heavily armoured ship, was greater than that of shellfire. How would these weapons affect two fleets equal in quality under the particular conditions of the North Sea? The possible consequences had been analysed and remedies sought in British annual manoeuvres since the 1880s, but it took the experience of war, with ships sunk and men killed, to establish the psychological impact on captains and admirals. Further uncertainties existed on the importance of submarines and the more recently developed aeroplanes and airships, as well as the adoption of wireless telegraphy. Would this latter give fleet commanders better control of their forces? Could the interception of enemy signals be an aid to location and interception? What would be the result of authorities ashore having the capability to issue orders to the commanders at sea? The significance of all these factors arising from technological change was unknown when, on 4 August 1914, the Royal Navy was ordered to begin hostilities against Germany.

NAVAL POLICY AND STRATEGY

The build-up of the German navy, beginning with the Naval Law of 1898, necessitated a reorientation of British naval strategy. Instead of the wide distribution of forces, especially in the Mediterranean, the major concentration had in future to be in the North Sea. As the former naval rivals, France and Russia, became allies and Britain's Far Eastern interests were secured by the 1902 alliance with Japan, the whole of the Royal Navy's thinking and dispositions centred on the defeat of Germany. This was translated into action by the determination of Sir John Fisher, First Sea Lord 1904–10. The whole of the modern battle fleet was concentrated in home waters. His conviction that heavy hitting and high speed combined were the necessary ingredients of success in battle produced the revolutionary capital ships, the Dreadnoughts, in both battleship and battle-cruiser form, which made all preceding types obsolete. This intensified the naval competition with a Germany determined to end Britain's domination of the seas, which it saw as an obstacle to both its imperial ambitions and the maintenance of its security in Europe. Despite diplomatic efforts to restrain it, the naval race intensified, with Britain determined to have a 60 per cent superiority in capital ships, and Germany equally determined to have a more even balance. Anglo-German naval rivalry was not the cause of the Great War, but it did ensure that when the continental rivalries of Germany and Austria with France and Russia led to conflict Britain could not stand aloof.

If it was clear to Fisher and the Royal Navy generally that its battleground would be the North Sea and that its aim would be an early decisive defeat of the High Seas Fleet, technological change had made it far less clear how such a fleet action could be brought about. The close blockade of enemy ports, which had been the hinge of naval strategy in the days of sail, had been rendered impossible by the emergence of mines, torpedo-boats and submarines capable of sinking the blockading fleet. This had been accepted by Britain in 1912 and was replaced gradually by a concept of distant blockade, in which heavy ships would be kept in harbour until warned by observational forces and other intelligence that the enemy was on the point of moving. This obviously meant a far greater possibility of the enemy escaping from harbour, carrying out minor operations, such as raids against the British coast and minelaying, and returning home before being intercepted.

If technology had changed the shape of naval warfare, the facts of geography remained. Britain's position relative to the Continent made it easy for her to close off the exits from the North Sea to enemy surface ships; submarines proved more difficult. In the Dover Strait light craft and physical barriers proved effective. In the north, cruiser squadrons, backed by the Grand Fleet in its nearby bases, effectively blocked access to the Atlantic (Map 3.1). Only a victory over the Grand Fleet could break the strategic and economic blockade of Germany which this implied.

TACTICAL FAILURES – STRATEGIC SUCCESS

If fleet superiority was the key to success, Britain clearly held it. In August 1914 she had twenty-four Dreadnought battleships, with eleven more building. Germany had fifteen with six building, three of which were never completed. In the faster battle-cruisers, Britain

Map 3.1: The North Sea Blockade, 1914–18

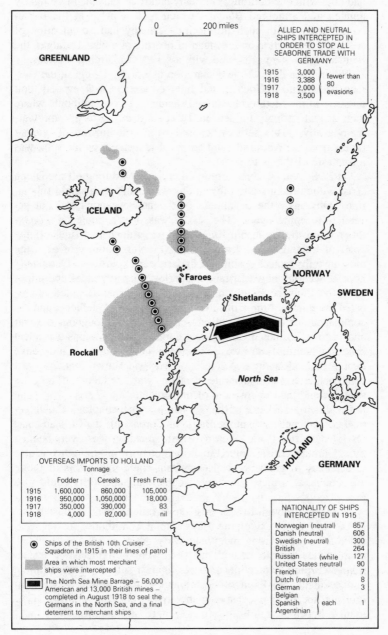

0   200 miles

GREENLAND

ICELAND

Faroes

Shetlands

NORWAY

SWEDEN

Rockall

North Sea

HOLLAND

GERMANY

ALLIED AND NEUTRAL SHIPS INTERCEPTED IN ORDER TO STOP ALL SEABORNE TRADE WITH GERMANY		
1915	3,000	fewer than 80 evasions
1916	3,388	
1917	2,000	
1918	3,500	

OVERSEAS IMPORTS TO HOLLAND
Tonnage

	Fodder	Cereals	Fresh Fruit
1915	1,600,000	860,000	105,000
1916	950,000	1,050,000	18,000
1917	350,000	390,000	83
1918	4,000	82,000	nil

⊙   Ships of the British 10th Cruiser Squadron in 1915 in their lines of patrol

▓   Area in which most merchant ships were intercepted

■   The North Sea Mine Barrage – 56,000 American and 13,000 British mines – completed in August 1918 to seal the Germans in the North Sea, and a final deterrent to merchant ships

NATIONALITY OF SHIPS INTERCEPTED IN 1915

Norwegian (neutral)		857
Danish (neutral)		606
Swedish (neutral)		300
British		264
Russian	(while	127
United States neutral)		90
French		7
Dutch (neutral		8
German		3
Belgian		
Spanish	each	1
Argentinian		

had nine with one building, Germany had four, plus the more lightly gunned and armoured *Blücher* which took a place in the battle-cruiser line. With such inferiority Germany had no intention of seeking a fleet action and, instead of hearing of a new Trafalgar, the British public were presented with a series of alarming reverses.

Within three days of the declaration of war on 4 August, the German battle-cruiser *Goeben* and light cruiser *Breslau* evaded their pursuers in the Mediterranean and steamed to Constantinople where their arrival strongly influenced Turkey's decision to become Germany's ally. This setback, caused by a combination of unclear orders from the Admiralty and errors of judgement on the spot, was a foretaste of things to come.

On 22 September three armoured cruisers patrolling off the Dutch coast without taking any precautions were sunk by a single submarine. Obviously the deadliness of the new weapons had not yet been fully appreciated. The lesson was driven home on 27 October when the battleship *Audacious* was mined and sunk off the coast of Ireland, again demonstrating the vulnerability of even the most heavily protected ships to underwater explosions. Germany's hope of wearing down Britain's superiority by torpedoes and mines could not now be lightly dismissed. This, once accepted, dominated the minds of the British commander-in-chief, Jellicoe, and the commander of the battle-cruiser force, Beatty, throughout the war and instilled in their planning and conduct of operations a prudent caution which in future was to decrease the likelihood of a decisive fleet action. A short experience of war had shown that the most significant effect of underwater weapons was a reduction of a fleet's strategic and tactical freedom of movement.

Convincing evidence of the German navy's technological and tactical competence came at the Battle of Coronel off the Chilean coast on 1 November 1914, when a British squadron was overwhelmed by a German cruiser force, superior not only in strength but also in accuracy of gunnery. Unless Britain could match this in future encounters, a further reduction of numerical superiority could well take place.

Disturbing though this succession of failures was, it must be set in the wider context of the Navy's total contribution to the war. Once the danger from underwater weapons was fully appreciated, counter-measures to defend the fleet were introduced. Constant mine-sweeping, protection of bases against submarine penetration, and adequate provision of destroyer escorts, combined with fast cruising speeds and evasive manoeuvres, effectively barred Germany's hopes of significant attrition by these weapons.

Numerical superiority enabled Britain to send two battle-cruisers to the South Atlantic without unacceptably weakening the Grand Fleet, and their victory over von Spee's cruisers at the Falkland Islands on 8 December cleared the distant seas of all concentrated German forces. This removed any threat to the safe transport of troops from Australia and New Zealand and left only isolated raiders to attack merchant shipping on the wider oceans.

In contrast to this, success in sweeping German merchant shipping from the seas, combined with the prevention of seaborne supplies in neutral ships reaching Germany were in the long term to prove a significant factor in her ultimate military and political collapse (Map 3.1). Furthermore, the preservation of Grand Fleet superiority ensured that Germany never successfully interrupted the continuous flow of men and materials across the Channel, essential to the ultimate success of the Allied armies, nor ever seriously planned the invasion of the British Isles. The English exponent of sea power, Sir Julian Corbett,[2] in his *Some Principles of Maritime Strategy*, had stressed that naval battles would never win major wars: the final decision had to be on land. The navy's role was to protect the home base, obtain and maintain use of the sea for military and economic purposes, and deny that use to the enemy. This contribution to overall victory was successfully made by the Royal Navy, although it very nearly failed in one respect.

THE SEARCH FOR A NAVAL OFFENSIVE – AMPHIBIOUS OPERATIONS

With an Admiralty headed by Winston Churchill, young and impulsive, as its political chief and the old but aggressive Admiral Fisher (recalled by Churchill to be First Sea Lord in October 1914), acceptance of a defensive role, however justified strategically, was unthinkable. Between them they produced a succession of proposals for amphibious operations in the Baltic and for the seizure of the German islands of Borkum and Heligoland. The former, especially if carried out in co-operation with Russia, would divert German resources from both the Eastern and Western Fronts, while the islands would provide advanced naval bases from which the German navy could be attacked by torpedo-craft. All such schemes were turned down. The navy argued that opposed landings in such waters would

2 J. S. Corbett, *Some Principles of Naval Strategy* (London: Longman, 1911). A new edition by the Naval Press (Annapolis, Md) is planned for 1987. D. M. Schurman (note 1 above) provides a sound evaluation of Corbett's work and significance.

fail because of the defensive weaponry available. The army agreed
and added its constant objections to any withdrawal of troops from
the Western Front.

The inspiration of the one major amphibious operation which was
attempted was Churchill's typically imaginative proposal to drive
Turkey out of the war by sending a fleet through the Dardanelles to
bombard Constantinople. The operation was backed by the Cabinet,
eager to find an alternative to the Western stalemate and to be able
to offer relief to an already struggling Russia. The army and navy
were less keen, and at first the army refused to provide any troops.
This led, in February and March 1915, to two unsuccessful attempts
to silence the guns defending the straits by naval gunfire alone. Lord
Kitchener, Secretary of State for War, having reluctantly agreed to
provide the troops, landings – successfully conducted – began on
25 April and were followed by others. But the troops, because of
unco-ordinated leadership, the nature of the terrain and, above all,
the stubborn Turkish resistance, were unable to attain their objective and were evacuated in January 1916. The total British Empire
and French casualties – dead, wounded and evacuated because of
sickness – were 250,000, a heavy price to pay for the lack of the
close inter-service co-operation and detailed planning which were
essential to success in joint operations.

THE SEARCH FOR A NAVAL OFFENSIVE – NORTH SEA RAIDS AND BATTLES, 1914–15

Throughout the war the Royal Navy hoped to fight a decisive action
with the High Seas Fleet, but early experience of the destructiveness
of mines and torpedoes convinced Jellicoe and Beatty, his battle-
cruiser commander and eventual successor, that this action must not
be sought in waters where minefields and submarines could seriously
reduce their numerical superiority. Germany, too, began to look for
a type of offensive appropriate to its relative strength and planned
for an opportunity to intercept a section of the Grand Fleet and
destroy it before superior forces could arrive to cut off their retreat
home. Confrontation with the whole of the Grand Fleet was to be
avoided until its numbers had been reduced by such an action added
to the effects of mines and torpedoes. Events at sea – the Battle of
Heligoland Bight, the German battle-cruiser raid on the east coast
and the Battle of the Dogger Bank (Map 3.2) – soon showed how
difficult it was to be for both sides to achieve their aims.

The first difficulty was location. Despite the Admiralty's possession of captured German code books and of its creation of an ef-

Map 3.2: North Sea Battles, 1914–18

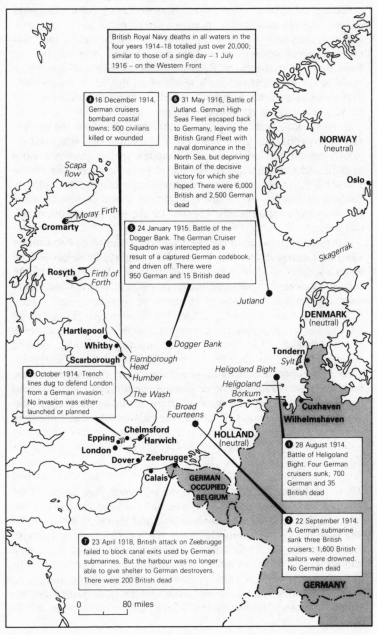

British Royal Navy deaths in all waters in the four years 1914–18 totalled just over 20,000; similar to those of a single day – 1 July 1916 – on the Western Front

❹ 16 December 1914, German cruisers bombard coastal towns; 500 civilians killed or wounded

❻ 31 May 1916, Battle of Jutland. German High Seas Fleet escaped back to Germany, leaving the British Grand Fleet with naval dominance in the North Sea, but depriving Britain of the decisive victory for which she hoped. There were 6,000 British and 2,500 German dead

❺ 24 January 1915. Battle of the Dogger Bank. The German Cruiser Squadron was intercepted as a result of a captured German codebook, and driven off. There were 950 German and 15 British dead

❸ October 1914. Trench lines dug to defend London from a German invasion. No invasion was either launched or planned

❶ 28 August 1914. Battle of Heligoland Bight. Four German cruisers sunk; 700 German and 35 British dead

❷ 22 September 1914. A German submarine sank three British cruisers; 1,600 British sailors were drowned. No German dead

❼ 23 April 1918, British attack on Zeebrugge failed to block canal exits used by German submarines. But the harbour was no longer able to give shelter to German destroyers. There were 200 British dead

NORWAY (neutral)

Oslo

Scapa flow

Moray Firth

Cromarty

Rosyth

Firth of Forth

Skagerrak

Jutland

DENMARK (neutral)

Tondern
Sylt

Hartlepool
Whitby
Scarborough
Flamborough Head
Humber
The Wash

Dogger Bank

Heligoland Bight
Heligoland
Borkum

Cuxhaven
Wilhelmshaven

Broad Fourteens

Chelmsford
Epping
London
Dover

Harwich
Zeebrugge

HOLLAND (neutral)

Calais

GERMAN OCCUPIED BELGIUM

GERMANY

0   80 miles

fective radio interception organization linked to the civilian-manned decoding and interpretation centre, 'Room 40', their information was never complete and the interpretations were liable to human error. Germany had no equivalent but relied on her Zeppelins for long-range reconnaissance. Success here depended on clear weather, far from frequent in the North Sea, and good communications, which could never be relied on. As a result of all this neither side could ever be certain of the strength in which its opponent was at sea, let alone of his precise position and future intentions.

Even if skill, luck and good weather brought about the desired encounter, variations in visibility could cause loss of contact and seriously impair gunnery accuracy. Weapons, shells, gunnery control systems and communications, subjected to battle conditions for the first time, might not live up to peacetime expectations. And, closely connected with this, it was likely that there would be human errors by commanders at all levels, exposed for the first time to the strains of battle.

All these factors inhibiting decisive fleet actions had become evident by January 1915. The Royal Navy retained its determination to seek a decision. But even its most aggressively minded admiral, Sir David Beatty, in all three operations was affected in his judgement by the real or imagined presence of submarines and mines. Although he was an inspiring leader, his battle-cruiser force showed weaknesses in reconnaissance, communications and gunnery which revealed that he had not yet succeeded in training it up to the required standards. The German admirals, von Ingenohl the commander-in-chief, and Hipper the battle-cruiser commander, although they must have been encouraged by their gunnery performance, were placed under such restrictions by their superiors, including the Kaiser himself, that they were unlikely to take the risks involved in forcing an action to a decisive conclusion.

JUTLAND, 31 MAY 1916

These inhibitions still prevailed at the one great fleet action of the war and were shared by Jellicoe, who had not been in tactical command in the three previous encounters, and Reinhard Scheer, who had been the German commander-in-chief only since January 1916. Also new was the size of the forces they had to control. Britain had some 150 ships, including 30 battleships and 9 battle-cruisers, Germany 101, with 22 battleships and 5 battle-cruisers. Jellicoe, a realistic and cautious man, well aware of the high qualities of the enemy's gunnery and haunted by fears of falling into a mine or submarine trap, and the man whom Churchill had described as being able to lose the war in an afternoon, was not going to take risks. Scheer, more offensively minded than his predecessors though he was, would never ignore his orders to avoid action with a superior force. He put to sea in the hope of encountering only a detachment of the Grand Fleet and was taken by surprise when faced by Jellicoe's whole force. Two other factors made the indecisive result of Jutland virtually a foregone conclusion: the visibility on the day represented the North Sea at its worst, and the Admiralty intelligence and staff system, although successful at first in bringing about the encounter, still had weaknesses.

Beatty succeeded in his main objective of leading the High Seas Fleet into the jaws of the Grand Fleet, which Scheer did not know to be at sea until he came under its gunfire. But while doing this the comparative weakness of British gunnery and armoured protection had been shown by the loss of two of Beatty's battle-cruisers, nor had his reconnaissance reports given Jellicoe accurate information on his opponent's position and course. Despite this, Jellicoe made the most important decision of his career by deploying his force in such a way as to bar the enemy from returning to base. In the resultant action, accurate Grand Fleet gunnery repelled two German attempts to break through the barrier. Scheer avoided severe losses by skilful turning-away manoeuvres which Jellicoe refused to follow up closely, fearing that he was being tempted into a mine and submarine trap. In the pursuit and sporadic night actions which followed, the chronic British weakness in reporting the enemy's position and course, and the even more serious Admiralty staff failure in not passing on to Jellicoe 'Room 40' information which would have enabled him to cut off the enemy on the morning of 1 June enabled Scheer to reach his base.

The comparative losses, of 14 British ships sunk and some 6,000 dead to the German 11 ships and some 2,500 dead, are evidence of the high accuracy of German gunnery and the relatively better performance of their shells and armoured protection. It was inevitable that Germany should claim a victory, and she had good reason to be proud of her fleet's performance. British public opinion was shocked at what appeared to be a serious and unexpected reverse. Yet, even in the short run, this was a false interpretation. The Germans had failed to end the Grand Fleet's numerical superiority. Its damaged ships were ready for action well before its opponents', and the lessons of the action were digested and fully put into effect by Beatty who succeeded Jellicoe in command in November 1916. As for the High Seas Fleet, it never sought action with the Grand Fleet again, making only limited sorties, and when it was ordered to make a final onslaught in October 1918 widespread mutiny prevented its sailing. With its enemy thus hemmed in the Grand Fleet had fulfilled its function, although deprived of its Trafalgar. As to the criticisms of Jellicoe's handling of Jutland, and the bitter controversy between himself and Beatty after the war, a quotation from his report to the Admiralty on 4 June 1916 puts his conduct and the whole nature of naval warfare at the time into perspective :

> The whole situation was so difficult to grasp as I had no real idea of what was going on, and we could hardly see anything except flashes of guns, shells falling, ships blowing up, and an occasional glimpse of an enemy vessel.[3]

UNRESTRICTED SUBMARINE WARFARE

Nowhere was the impact of technological change more apparent than in Germany's operations against merchant shipping. Such operations had always figured in maritime war, designed to exert such economic pressure on an opponent as to make him seek peace. They had never been decisive against Britain, whose general naval strength had kept losses to an acceptable level. But in the Great War there were two new elements. Britain had become totally dependent for food and raw materials on the regular arrival of vast numbers of merchant ships, and in the submarine Germany had found a weapon undeterred by surface superiority.

The use of the submarine in this way had not been foreseen by any major naval figure except Admiral Fisher, and he had failed to convince British politicians that he was right. It was thought that no civilized power would risk the obloquy from the deaths of passengers and crews that would ensue. German naval opinion itself had not seriously considered the option before the war. But as the U-boats proved their sea endurance, and as the land war moved towards stalemate, both naval and military leaders began to overcome the objections of the civil authorities. From February 1915 there were periods of attacks without warning on neutral as well as Allied ships,

3 Jellicoe to A. J. Balfour (First Lord of the Admiralty), 4 June 1916, Ministry of Defence (Navy) Library, Earls Court, Jackson Papers. The most complete treatment of Jutland is in A. J. Marder, *From the Dreadnought to Scapa Flow*, Vol. 3, *Jutland and After*, revised edn (Oxford: Oxford University Press, 1978). Jellicoe's *The Grand Fleet* (London: Cassell, 1919), pp. 354 ff., describes his difficulties.

alternating with withdrawals in response to the protests of the United States and other neutrals. But by the beginning of 1917, the German high command, accepting its inability to win a prolonged war, finally convinced the government that if all merchant shipping were subject to attack Britain would be defeated within six months. To achieve this it was necessary to accept the risk that the United States would enter the war, which of course it did.

Even before this final onslaught Britain's situation was critical. Well over a million tons of shipping had been lost in 1916 and, unless a remedy could soon be found, the German claim might well be confirmed. As the losses of ships had increased, the Admiralty had allocated a force of some 4,000 vessels, supplemented by aircraft and mines, to anti-submarine tasks, but their successes were far overtaken by the German building programme. By the spring of 1917, one in four ships coming to Britain was being sunk and only about nine weeks' grain supply was left in the country. Yet when the American Admiral Sims asked Jellicoe if there was a solution in sight the First Sea Lord replied: 'Absolutely none that we can see at present.'[4]

Yet a solution was at hand in the form of the convoy system which Jellicoe and the majority of naval authorities rejected, mainly on the grounds that a collection of ships would be far easier to find and destroy than would ships sailing separately. This was a virtually unchallenged dogma which, along with the fact that ship-owners were strongly opposed to the total control of their property required for convoy, had prevented an impartial investigation of the subject. This would have revealed that the primary problem of locating the submarine could not be solved by the existing method of searching wide areas of sea. The only location instruments available, hydrophones to pick up the submarines' sound-waves, were simply not effective enough. But if the search area were radically reduced to that in which a submarine must operate to have a reasonable chance of hitting its target, then success was much more likely, especially if escorts were on the spot to drop the depth charges which were becoming available in adequate quantity. This was achieved by the convoy system which also prevented the surface gunfire attacks which submarines had been able to use against single ships.

It was only the sheer desperation of 1917 and the pressure of a number of naval officers, including Beatty, which in April overcame Jellicoe's opposition. It took months to organize a complete convoy system but losses began to decline in the summer. When the system

4 W.S. Sims, *The Victory at Sea* (London: Murray, 1920), pp. 6–7.

was complete the results were startling. Between February and October 1918, of the some 16,000 ships sailing in ocean convoy, only 96 were sunk; in coastal convoys, only 161 out of a total of 68,000.

That the Admiralty took so long to reach a solution is the strongest criticism of the Royal Navy's performance in the war. It does not mean that the men concerned were stupid, although characteristically of their profession and status they were dogmatic in adhering to long established positions. The failure is best seen as the most illuminating example of the underlying difficulty faced by the naval profession throughout the war – the impossibility of assessing the precise impact of technological change until it has actually been put to the test of battle.

THE HUMAN FACTOR

If the *matériel* of the German navy at least equalled that of its rival, its personnel did not. That Germany's war at sea ended in mutiny and collapse of morale was both the cause and the explanation of her defeat. Her naval officer corps had adopted some of the army's worst characteristics. It was professionally competent but rigid and aloof in its relationship with the men and, generally, paid little attention to their welfare. The mutinies of 1918 which destroyed the High Seas Fleet as a fighting force were affected by Germany's military reverses, political disintegration and the revolutionary agitation arising from it, but their primary cause was internal unrest. Harsh discipline and poor conditions which might have been tolerated in a victorious force proved fatal to one condemned to inactivity by its leaders' negative strategy. In contrast, the morale of the submarine force remained high.

The Royal Navy, too, was a hierarchical organization based on discipline and privilege and sprung from a still deferential society. It was manned by volunteers, most of whom had entered at the age of 15–16 and then, at 18, signed on for a minimum of twelve years. Instructed by petty officers who had been through the same mill, they took for granted a discipline and control of their lives quite unthinkable today. The question was whether this system could adapt itself to changing social conditions and the wider fields of recruitment which technological development and massive wartime expansion necessitated (Table 3.1). Isolated though the navy was, its men could not have been unaware of the political radicalism and trade-union struggles for better pay and conditions which characterized the early years of the twentieth century. That such potential causes of disaffection did not undermine discipline and readiness to

Map 3.3: The Western Approaches, 1914–18

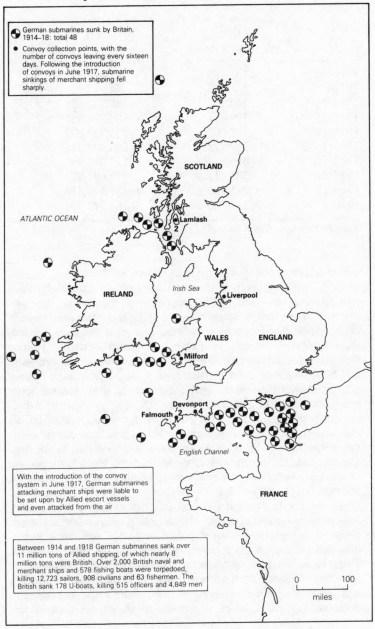

German submarines sunk by Britain, 1914–18: total 48

Convoy collection points, with the number of convoys leaving every sixteen days. Following the introduction of convoys in June 1917, submarine sinkings of merchant shipping fell sharply.

SCOTLAND

ATLANTIC OCEAN

Lamlash 2

IRELAND

Irish Sea

7 Liverpool

WALES

ENGLAND

4 Milford

Devonport

Falmouth 2

English Channel

With the introduction of the convoy system in June 1917, German submarines attacking merchant ships were liable to be set upon by Allied escort vessels and even attacked from the air

FRANCE

Between 1914 and 1918 German submarines sank over 11 million tons of Allied shipping, of which nearly 8 million tons were British. Over 2,000 British naval and merchant ships and 578 fishing boats were torpedoed, killing 12,723 sailors, 908 civilians and 63 fishermen. The British sank 178 U-boats, killing 515 officers and 4,849 men

0   100

miles

Table 3.1   *Naval manpower and expenditure, 1911–20*

	Average Number of Officers and Men Borne	Total expenditure (£s)
1911–12	132,792	42,414,257
1912–13	136,443	44,933,169
1913–14	142,960	48,732,621
1914–15	199,451	103,301,862
1915–16	297,008	205,733,597
1916–17	349,578	209,877,218
1917–18	406,977	227,388,891
1918–19	381,311	334,091,277
1919–20	275,000	157,528,810
1920–1	136,000	84,372,300

Source: *Brassey's Naval Annual*, 1920–1

accept authority was due to the navy's own reforms.

At the working level, officers and petty officers, themselves becoming more technically skilled, realized that the handling of complex machinery and weapons required skills and adaptability which could not be developed by a bullying type of leadership. Second, the majority of officers, themselves committed to the navy since they were 13, although confident of their unquestionable authority, had been taught to exert it paternalistically, in the sense of being concerned with their men's well-being and, off duty, seeking some common ground in games and recreation. The example of Admiral Beatty at the summit of the hierarchy, providing turkeys for his men's Christmas dinner, encouraging his wife to help sailors' families and, despite all his other responsibilities, deliberately taking time to make himself clearly visible throughout the Fleet by appearing at sporting events and concerts, was symbolic of what he expected, and was largely achieved, in every ship.

It must not be thought from all this that the navy was a naturally progressive and benevolent organization. Resistance to change, abuse of authority and sheer stupidity are part of the human condition, and there are many reasons why they flourish in armed forces. To prevent their figuring to an unacceptable extent necessitates reform and vigilance from the top. That these came before the war was the third factor in ensuring that the sense of all belonging to one company, the basis of all fighting spirit, was well established in the Royal Navy. It was fortunate that the two men most influential in preparing it for war – Admiral Sir John Fisher and Winston Churchill, its political head since 1911 – were as much aware of the human factor as they were of the demands of strategy and technology. They both saw themselves as radical reformers, determined to remedy grievances in discipline, pay and living conditions which obstructed an increasingly educated and more socially aware lower deck from maintaining the loyalty and enthusiasm necessary for success in the long and frustrating war which lay ahead. By 1912 the basic changes had been made and, although some further grievances surfaced during the war, and more widespread ones at its end, there was never any likelihood of the collapse of morale which led the High Seas Fleet to surrender and internment. However revolutionary the effects of technological development had been, in the last resort victory still went to the side with the more effective leadership and the higher morale.

4

The New Warfare and Economic Mobilization

PETER DEWEY

INTRODUCTION

The war which became known as the First World War was rather more limited than the title suggests. The only major non-European belligerent was the United States of America, which did not enter the war until 1917. For most of its course, the war was essentially a European civil war, in which the main combatants were France, Germany, Britain, Russia and Italy.

The Eurocentric nature of the war had a vital consequence: it meant that the conflict was between industrialized nations. The first nation to industrialize had been Britain, which commenced the process some time in the late eighteenth century. She was followed into the industrial age by other countries in northern and western Europe and by the United States of America. The principal industrial economies on the Continent by 1914 were Belgium, Germany and France.[1] Industrialization had important consequences. First, it led for the first time in history to a long-term rise in average living standards, such that for a large part (although by no means all) of the population, the gap between income and subsistence widened perceptibly. Second, industrialization led, especially after 1870, to the large-scale development of certain industries which were of particular importance for contemporary warfare. These were centred on the production of metals, engineering and chemicals. Among them, the steel industry may serve as a general illustration: in 1871, the combined production of the five main belligerents was only 0.6 million

1 For the British Industrial Revolution, see P. Mathias, *The First Industrial Nation* 2nd edn (London: Methuen, 1983); for the European, C. Trebilcock, *The Industrialisation of the Continental Powers* (London: Longman, 1981).

tonnes; in 1913 this had risen to 32.7 million tonnes. The Industrial Revolution was accompanied by population growth at an unprecedented rate; the 'population explosion' of the nineteenth century was above all a European affair. In 1800 the five main belligerents had a combined population of about 69.8 million; by 1910 this had risen fivefold, to 355.5 million.[2]

The potential military implications of this century of revolutionary economic change were that much larger armies could be raised; they could be supplied on a much greater scale with the products of industry; the tax-paying ability of the average citizen was greatly enhanced; and civilians could be subject to considerable reductions in their living standards before being reduced to mere subsistence.

Thus the potential for waging war on a much bigger scale than in earlier times was a product of these economic changes. That this potential was translated into reality was due to the accompanying changes in the nature of military technology, which were a product of developments in steel, engineering and chemicals in the late nineteenth century.

In military terms, there were many changes by 1914. Thus the universal infantry weapon had become the rapid-fire rifle, which had a magazine of six to eight rounds; when trained, riflemen could consistently achieve a rate of fire of fifteen rounds per minute.[3] In addition, the propellants used were much more powerful, so that the range of action was considerably increased. More potently, the machine-gun had been refined so as greatly to increase its killing power: the Vickers gun, the most widely used in the British army, had a range of 2,900 yards, a rate of fire of eight rounds per second, and a magazine of 250 rounds.[4] Troops could also now reinforce their positions with barbed wire, first used on the cattle ranches of America. But perhaps the greatest technological change centred on the development of high explosive. This, which replaced the black powder which armies had used for centuries, dates from Alfred Nobel's use of nitro-glycerine to produce dynamite (1866). He followed this up in 1888 by producing a propellant with a controlled rate of burning.[5] Other explosives and propellants were subsequently discovered by chemists in Germany, Britain and France, so that by

2 See B. R. Mitchell, *European Historical Statistics* (London: Macmillan, 1975), pp. 20–1, 400–1.

3 John Terraine, *White Heat: The New Warfare 1914–18* (London: Sidgwick & Jackson, 1982), p. 80.

4 C. M. Beadnell, *An Encyclopaedic Dictionary of Science and War* (London: Watts, 1943), pp. 272–3.

5 L. F. Haber, *The Chemical Industry during the Nineteenth Century*

1914 heavy artillery in the modern sense had come into being. This comprised, not merely long-range artillery, but a variety of types, including short-range howitzers and mortars, with a choice of high-explosive or shrapnel shell.[6]

Military changes were echoed in naval warfare. Here there were two main developments: the heavy battleship, such as *Dreadnought* (1906), which was essentially a heavily armoured, high-speed gun platform, and the submarine, which by 1914 had developed into an efficient long-range weapon for sinking surface vessels.

One further general change affected the way in which land warfare was conducted: the spread of the railway had by 1914 permitted armies to be mobilized much more quickly than in earlier wars. In addition, it greatly facilitated the switching of troops from one front to another, even in winter, when poor ground conditions had traditionally hampered mobility.

The outbreak of war in 1914 thus took place against a technical background that was radically different from that of earlier centuries. Taken in conjunction with the early tactical developments on the Western Front, the result was a stalemate that lasted for four years. This was not foreseen at the time; the German battle plan (named after its originator, Count von Schlieffen) aimed for a quick knockout blow on the French armies, delivered through (neutral) Belgian territory. The plan, however, foundered through a combination of poor generalship and Allied resistance; both sides dug in, and the war of the trenches began.

The war of mobility in the west being over, both sides had recourse to dug-out positions of increasing complexity. The military novelties cited above came into their own, and proved to have one thing in common which was to dominate trench warfare: they gave a large advantage to the defence. Trenches protected with forward emplacements of barbed wire and sandbags, occupied by soldiers with rapid-fire rifles and with machine-guns were very difficult to storm. Commanders on both sides took a long time to appreciate this. When they did, it seemed that a way out of the impasse might be through the use of heavy artillery, which could be employed to weaken the entrenched enemy (and his artillery) before the attack began, and provide a cover under which the first troops might begin their advance. Once begun, the attack could be facilitated by an

(Oxford: Oxford University Press, 1958), pp. 90–1.

6 e.g., the lists of munitions in Part 7 of the War Office publication, *Statistics of the Military Effort of the British Empire during the Great War 1914–20* (London: HMSO, 1922), hereafter referred to as SME.

advancing curtain of shells in the form of the 'creeping barrage', although this required very accurate fire. However, massed infantry attack supported by artillery proved to have a great disadvantage: it churned up the terrain and destroyed roadways and paths so as to make future movement of men and supplies next to impossible. That apart, the new warfare proved to be immensely prodigal of human life and material, and failed in its main aim: to capture ground. The first major British offensive of the war, the battle of Neuve Chapelle in March 1915, lasted three days and led to an advance of only 1,200 yards on a front of 4,000 yards, at a cost of 13,000 British and 12,000 German casualties.

This extraordinary, novel and wasteful military stalemate continued for almost four years; commanders seemed impotent to break the deadlock, although many expedients were tried. Yet technical change, which had engendered this system, did not provide the answer. Perhaps the greatest weakness of the attack lay in the lack of communication once it had begun. Commanders in the trenches were almost powerless to communicate with their advancing troops. Telephones were used, but depended on wires, which were vulnerable, so that armies fell back on hand signals or runners, both of which were unreliable and dangerous. Other expedients such as mining were widely used by both sides, but were never decisive. Nor were wartime technical developments of much help: aeroplanes and balloons were useful for observation rather than for offence, and the tank was never deployed in large enough numbers to be decisive. The land stalemate was paralleled by the stalemate at sea; the British and German fleets avoided each other for most of the war, only coming together in the indecisive engagement at Jutland in May 1916. The German submarine fleet caused much damage to shipping in 1917–18, but did not cripple the British war effort, and its effects were replicated by the British blockade of the north German coast.[7]

The nature of the war for Britain was thus determined by military technology and the deadlock on the Western Front. Given these elements, the main economic task in wartime was to find manpower, munitions and money. These needs are common to all economies at war; what was new was the sheer scale of the effort required, such that economic and social life came to be dominated by the war. This scale was only apparent in the course of time. Had it been apparent initially, much waste would have been avoided; the

---

7 For this and the preceding paragraphs, see Terraine, *White Heat*, pp. 34–8, 45–8, 100–10, 142–9.

government could have allocated men and materials in accordance with an overall economic strategy. This may be contrasted with the experience of the Second World War, where eventually (although not until 1942) a central manpower budget was evolved, covering both military and civilian labour. This made it much easier to plan for the production of goods for military and civilian use.[8] As it was, in the First World War most economic policies were reactions to specific problems rather than long-term strategies.

MANPOWER

In no area was this more true than in that of manpower. Here, the crucial question was the size of the army, and thus the residual labour available for industry and commerce. To most people's surprise, over a million men answered Lord Kitchener's initial appeal for recruits before the end of 1914, and by the end of 1915 the army stood at 2.5 million. Fearing that voluntary enlistment was losing its appeal, the government introduced conscription in 1916, and with its aid the final size of the army reached some 3.8 million.[9]

That the British population could yield an army of this size had hardly been contemplated before the war. Yet the very success with which the military recruitment target was met gave rise to the other main manpower problem, that of an adequate supply of labour for the rest of the economy. This was made worse by the fact that the pattern of labour loss as between different industries, which was determined in the first two years of the war, was not necessarily one which matched the nature of wartime labour demand. By July 1916 the national average labour loss due to recruiting was 30 per cent. This was also the loss shown in the manufacturing and mining sector, but there were considerable variations in other sectors, from the 41 per cent recorded in commerce to as little as 22 per cent in agriculture. (Table 4.1)

The high labour loss in the commercial sector was notable, but was not such a hindrance to the war effort as the loss of labour in manufacturing and mining, which faced enormously increased demands for their products from the military. The earliest and most dramatic example of this came in May 1915, when the 'shell scandal', with its allegations of shortages and poor quality, took the

8 W. K. Hancock and M.M. Gowing, *British War Economy* (London: HMSO, 1949), pp. 48 ff.
9 In March 1918. This refers to British soldiers; including colonial and other troops, the figure for the British Empire was 5.6 million (SME, pp. 33–5).

Table 4.1   *Enlistment in the armed forces by occupational sector, as a percentage of male employment in July 1914*

	To July 1916 (per cent)	To July 1918 (per cent)
Manufacturing and mining	30	45
Agriculture	22	35
Transport	23	38
Commerce, finance and services	41	63
Public services	27	39
National average	30	46

Source: Board of Trade, *Report on the State of Employment in the United Kingdom* ... (July 1916 and July 1918). These reports, most of which were not published, are analysed in P. E. Dewey, 'Military recruiting and the British labour force during the First World War', *Historical Journal*, vol. 27, no. 1 (1984).

government by surprise. The upshot of this was the founding of the first of the new war ministries, the Ministry of Munitions, which was a much more efficient organization for the purpose than the many competing firms and industries which until then had been responsible for the supply of munitions.

Reorganization, however, would not by itself solve the problem. The main solution could only be found by expanding the labour supply. Here, the best-known example is that of female labour. Ultimately, an extra 1.6 million women entered the war economy, and about half of these were employed in manufacturing. Thus the public became accustomed to the idea of women working on the factory floor, and doing a great variety of jobs which before the war had been considered as either too heavy, too dangerous or too degrading for women to perform. As well as taking part on a large scale, for the first time, in the mechanical and chemical engineering industries, women played a large part in the transport, commercial and service sectors, the last two of which had suffered most of all from losses of labour to the forces.

The fact that the largest absolute increase in female labour was in manufacturing (largely munitions) should not obscure the fact that about half of the increase in the female labour supply went into other, mainly non-war industries. In particular, it is notable that over 400,000 went into commercial and financial work. This proved to be one of the few gains in women's employment that did not disappear at the end of the war; the male clerk with the copperplate handwriting was replaced by the female ledger clerk and shorthand-typist.

The increase in female labour was slightly less than the increase in male labour. By July 1918 male employment stood at 8.1 million, whereas four years previously it had been 10.6 million – a fall of 2.5 million. Yet in that time 4.9 million men had been withdrawn from the labour force for the Army (Table 4.2). Thus about 2.4 million men had been drawn into the war economy. However, a proportion of these were men returned from the forces, so that the net inflow of males into the labour force was rather less than 2.4 million. The Board of Trade estimated that roughly 700,000 men had returned to civilian employment from the forces by July 1918, so in effect the net influx of males into the labour force was only 1.7 million.[10]

Table 4.2   *Labour in the United Kingdom,*
             1914–18 (millions)

	Army recruitment	Civilian employment Males	Civilian employment Females	Total civilian employment
July:				
1914	0	10.6	3.3	13.9
1915	2.2	9.4	3.7	13.8
1916	3.2	8.9	4.2	13.1
1917	4.3	8.3	4.7	13.1*
1918	4.9	8.1	4.9	13.0

* rounding error
    Source: as Table 4.1

That the extra male labour drawn into the war economy exceeded the female labour may occasion some surprise, until the size of the male labour flow is realized. Thus the 'natural increase' of the male labour force in peacetime through school leavers entering employment was some 600,000 a year.[11] In addition, the wartime

10 Board of Trade, *Report on the State of Employment in All Occupations in the United Kingdom in July 1918* (unpublished), p.8.
11 B. R. Mitchell and P. Deane, *Abstract of British Historical Statistics* (Cambridge: Cambridge University Press, 1971), pp. 12–13.

labour supply was boosted by the virtual cessation of emigration, which before the war ran at about 200,000 (net) a year.[12] Finally, the male labour force was boosted by the postponement of retirement, boys being employed earlier than usual, and the virtual ending of unemployment.[13]

The end result was that the total civilian labour force was only marginally depleted. Whereas total employment in July 1914 has been estimated at 13.9 million (10.6 million men and 3.3 million women), it was thought in July 1918 to be 13.0 million (8.1 million men and 4.9 million women), a net loss of only 0.9 million (or some 6.5 per cent). When it is taken into account that there were at that time some 3.6 million British men in the army, it will be realized that the total labour force, both civilian and military, was much larger than before the war (Table 4.2).

MUNITIONS

The fairly successful maintenance of the civilian labour supply was one factor assisting the economy to cope with the twin pressures of the loss of labour and the need to supply the forces with war material. The other main factor was the way in which the economy shifted its structure so as to adapt to the enlarged demands of trench warfare. These demands were considerable from the beginning, and rose by many times during the war. Thus, to take one of the most crucial products, that of shells, some 2 million rounds had been sent to the Expeditionary Force in France by early April 1915. The subsequent founding of the Ministry of Munitions, which led to a considerable expansion in the number of directly controlled government shell factories, and of the orders placed on its behalf with private suppliers, led to an enormous rise in output; by the end of the war some 187 million rounds had been sent to France.[14]

The military effort also led to the rise of products which were hardly in evidence before the war. This may be illustrated by the annual production of machine guns (Table 4.3). The machine-gun might indeed serve as a useful symbol of the nature of warfare in 1914-18: a horridly efficient instrument for killing large numbers of men in the shortest possible time. Yet concentration on such sophisticated weapons might lead one to ignore the fact that the war

12 J. M. Winter, *The Great War and the British People* (London: Macmillan, 1985), p.266.
13 See n. 10 above.
14 SME, pp. 434–5.

Table 4.3   *British machine-gun output, 1914–18*

1914	274
1915	6,064
1916	33,200
1917	79,438
1918	120,864

Source: D. Lloyd George, *War Memoirs,* Vol. 1 (London: Odhams, 1938), p. 364.

also demanded large amounts of supplies of mundane kinds, and that this involved many industries not normally thought of in the same context as munitions factories. At the level of basic human need was clothing, provided in quantities which almost defy the imagination (Table 4.4).

Table 4.4   *British military clothing and footwear orders,*
             1914–18 (millions)

Boots	45	Puttees	35
Jackets	33	Shirts	55
Trousers	33	Drawers	70
Caps	26	Socks (pairs)	137
		Vests	22

Source: War Office, *Statistics of the Military Effort of the British Empire*, p.538

When it is realized that the maximum strength of the British and Empire forces was 5.6 million in March 1918, it is clear that they were at least adequately, if not excessively provided for in this respect. Clothing was not the end of the matter. A wide range of products, from the humdrum to the exotic, were required, and contracts for their supply flowed to manufacturers in large numbers throughout the war. The list of contracts awarded in July 1917 included orders for the supply of: 'Accoutrements, leather; Apparatus, shower bath; Bags, sleeping; Bandages, horse; Bells, electric; Buckets, canvas; Buzzers, practice; Cleavers; Cordage; Couches, X-ray; Covers, mess-tin; Disinfectants; Enamelled-ware; Flycatchers....'[15]

Thus the demands of the war economy were not limited to the more obvious war material. They were also inflated by the usual factor of military wastefulness. This sometimes took forms which

15 Board of Trade, *Supplement* to *Labour Gazette* (London: HMSO, August 1917), pp. 1–3.

would have surprised munitions workers. As Robert Graves observed: 'You would be surprised at the amount of waste that goes on in trenches. Ration biscuits are in general use as fuel for boiling up dixies, because fuel is scarce. Our machine-gun crews boil their hot water by firing off belt after belt of machine-gun ammunition at no particular target, just generally spraying the German line.'[16]

The multiplicity of demands made upon the economy meant that a large proportion of industry, and not just the obvious trades such as metals and chemicals, was geared to war work. To be sure, these two were the most heavily involved; by the last summer of the war, 90 per cent of labour in the entire metals industry and 79 per cent of labour in chemicals was on war work. But over half of labour in the wood industries was also on war work, as was 43 per cent in mining and quarrying, 41 per cent in building, 26 per cent in clothing, 20 per cent in paper and printing, and 13 per cent in the food, drink and tobacco trades. Overall, out of a male industrial labour force of some 5,165,000, some 3,132,500 were by this time engaged on war work, for either the British or the Allied governments: a ratio of 61 per cent.[17]

Even with the larger labour force, it was unlikely that so much of the productive effort of the nation could have gone to military ends without a reduction in civilian living standards. This in fact did occur, but only marginally. Thus consumers' expenditure, which was £3,522 million in 1913, had fallen to £2,819 million in 1918 (at constant prices), a fall of 20 per cent. A quarter of this decline was due to a fall in expenditure on food, a quarter on clothing, and a third on alcohol (Table 4.5). However, the nutritional value of the average diet was almost the same as before the war,[18] and the reduction of alcohol consumption was a positive benefit to the consumer, both nutritionally and financially. Only in the case of clothing could there be said to have been notable deprivation. However, such methods of measuring living standards do not take into account any deterioration in quality, and there is no doubt that the quality of certain items fell. This was particularly true of housing, where wartime overcrowding led to a rise in tubercular infection.[19]

Taken as a whole, the degree of hardship suffered by the nation

---

16 Robert Graves, *Goodbye to All That* (London: Cape, 1929), p. 150.
17 Winter, *Great War*, pp. 46–7.
18 P. E. Dewey, 'Food consumption in the United Kingdom, 1914–18', in R. Wall and J. M. Winter (eds), *The Upheaval of War* (Cambridge: Cambridge University Press, 1987).
19 Winter, *Great War*, p. 139.

Table 4.5   *Consumers' expenditure in the United Kingdom,
             1913–18 (£ million at 1910–13 prices)*

	Food	Alcohol and tobacco	Rents	Clothing	Other	Totals
1913	993	605	337	391	1,196	3,522
1914	994	597	342	336	1,177	3,446
1915	969	586	343	363	1,173	3,434
1916	908	526	343	253	1,101	3,131
1917	836	393	344	236	1,030	2,839
1918	829	382	346	226	1,035	2,819

Source: B. R. Mitchell and P. Deane, *Abstract of British Historical Statistics*
(Cambridge: Cambridge University Press, 1971), p. 371.

was not large, in spite of the fact that the labour force in manufacturing working to supply civilian needs was only about a third of what it had been before the war. Two reasons may be suggested for this; first, many 'inessential' trades were curtailed, either through market forces or through government action. Second, the larger pressure of demand relative to labour supply, both in war and non-war industries, stimulated a search for greater efficiency. Taken together, these factors, in the words of a Board of Trade report, permitted 'an almost unbelievable expenditure of effort on the war without this entailing any large amount of suffering to the civilian population'.[20]

MONEY

There were two main aspects to the money problem facing the government during the war. First, there was the task of raising money through taxation or other means to pay for the conduct of the war. Second, there was the external exchange aspect; here the problem was to ensure that there was enough foreign currency available to the government to pay for purchases of war material abroad, chiefly from the United States of America, and to maintain the exchange rate of the pound sterling.

The ability of the government to pay for the war by current taxation was strictly limited; like all belligerent nations, the British found that the war was so costly that it far outstripped the ability of the tax system to cope with it; the result was that the vast bulk of

20 Board of Trade, *Report on the State of Employment in…July 1918*, p.
    14.

the wartime expenditure was met by borrowing, that is, by increasing the National Debt. The extent of the shortfall in taxation can be seen by comparing wartime expenditure with total tax receipts (Table 4.6).

Table 4.6   *United Kingdom government expenditure and revenue, 1914–18 (£ million)*

	Expenditure	Tax revenue
1913	192	198
1914	559	227
1915	1,559	337
1916	2,198	573
1917	2,696	707
1918	2,579	889

Source: Mitchell and Deane, *Abstract*, pp. 394, 398.

Overall, only 30 per cent of expenditure was covered by taxation, so that 70 per cent remained to be added to the National Debt through sales of government bonds. This apparently low ratio was in fact the best performance of all the European powers – a further indication of the massive economic strain of the new warfare. The next best performance was that of France (24 per cent). Germany only managed 14 per cent, and the less developed countries of Eastern Europe generally did even worse.[21]

Some of the shortfall could doubtless have been avoided by a more vigorous tax policy, but successive Chancellors of the Exchequer could point out that increases in indirect taxation in wartime were politically unpopular; that direct taxation (chiefly income tax) had been considerably increased, so that on the whole the war had been fought on the principle that those who could afford most contributed most to the finance of the war; that a substantial new war tax, Excess Profits Duty, had been imposed on industry; and that in real terms the total tax-yield had more than doubled during the war.[22] On the whole, the problem was outside the control of the government, and rested upon the technological imperatives of the new warfare, which at its peak in 1916–17 meant that government expenditure accounted

21 Mitchell, *European Historical Statistics*, pp. 700, 719.
22 Sidney Pollard, *The Development of the British Economy, 1914–1980*, 3rd edn (London: Edward Arnold, 1983), pp. 30–2.

for 57–58 per cent of national income (GNP), as compared to about 7 per cent in 1913.[23] This made it inevitable that most of the war's cost would fall on the postwar taxpayer. In so far as this procedure strained the economy during the war itself, the strain was felt in rising prices; by the end of the war the price level had roughly doubled, and inflation had reached annual rates which far exceeded those of the last great inflationary period, the wars of 1793–1815 (Table 4.7).

Table 4.7   *Consumer price inflation, 1790–1814 and 1914–18*

Consumers' goods price index, 1790–1814 (1701=100)	
1790–4	126
1795–9	151
1800–4	186
1805–9	195
1810–14	220
Ministry of Labour Retail Price Index, 1914–18 (July 1914=100)	
1915	123
1916	146
1917	176
1918	203

Source: Mitchell and Deane, *Abstract*, pp. 469, 478.

The maintenance of the supply of necessary foreign exchange and the exchange value of the pound sterling were matters over which the government had little greater control. Here, the most influential factor was the size of the balance of payments surplus, derived from visible trade (goods) and invisible trade (services, including investment income). Before the war, Britain habitually had a deficit on visible trade, which was more than offset by a surplus on invisibles, thus leaving a net surplus on current account, which was usually reinvested abroad. Through this procedure, Britain had become the largest investor in the world, with foreign investments that may be conservatively estimated at £3,000 million.

During the war, the deficit in visible trade increased considerably, as export industries switched over to the war effort and the war closed many markets to British goods. At the same time, the volume of imports was maintained in real terms owing to the need to import

23 Mitchell and Deane, *Abstract*, pp. 368, 398. However, they describe the 1914–18 GNP figures as 'very rough'.

food and raw materials for civilians (as before 1914) and to provide
munitions and machines for the war effort (chiefly from the United
States of America). Thus the visible deficit, aided by inflation, rose
rapidly. This was mostly offset by a rise in the invisible surplus,
largely owing to the shortage of shipping, and thus high profits from
the hiring out of ships. The net result was that, whereas the surplus
on current account in 1913 had been £181 million, during the war the
entire surplus amounted to only £251 million, or about £50 million
a year on average (Table 4.8).

Table 4.8:   *United Kingdom balance of payments,
1914–18 (£ million)*

	Visible trade balance	Invisible trade balance	Current balance
1914	−170	+315	+145
1915	−368	+395	+27
1916	−345	+520	+175
1917	−467	+575	+108
1918	−784	+580	−204

Source: Sidney Pollard, *The Development of the British Economy, 1914–1980*,
3rd edn (London: Edward Arnold, 1983), p. 38.

Thus although the underlying balance of payments was weaker,
there was still a surplus to protect the sterling exchange rate. In so
far as there was a specific exchange problem, it lay in the need to
find American dollars. This was solved in part by raising loans in
America, and partly by taking measures to force British holders of
American securities to sell them and make the dollar proceeds over
to the Treasury. Thus bolstered, the exchange rate was held between
$4.76 and $4.77 from January 1916 to February 1919, although there
were some nasty moments, including a sterling crisis in early 1917.[24]

CONCLUSION

The problems which faced the British economy in the First World
War were essentially those of adapting human and economic resources to meet the demands of a new type of warfare which de-
voured men, munitions and money at an unprecedented rate. In this

24 Pollard, *Development*, p. 37.

process of adjustment, the formative influences were patriotism and economic forces. By the time that these were supplemented by state action, the shape of the war economy had been largely determined, in terms of such crucial matters as the size of the armed forces and the size of the industrial sector which supplied them with war material. Of the three items crucial for the prosecution of the war economy, money was in a sense the least essential (as long as the government's credit held good), given that most of the money cost of the war was shifted on to the postwar taxpayer. Only perhaps in the case of American dollars could it be said that money was essential for the continuance of the war. During the conflict, it was of greater importance to ensure that adequate supplies of labour for the forces and civilian industry were forthcoming, and that adequate production for both military and civilian use was available. In economic affairs, as in purely military, command of physical resources was what really counted.

5
The British Population at War

NOEL WHITESIDE

The impact of 'total war' between 1914 and 1918 transformed the face of British society. The scale of the conflict was quite unprecedented. The constant demand for men and munitions at the Front revolutionized the nature of the economy and the organization of the labour market, and led to an enormous expansion of state powers to manage the war effort. The old Edwardian order was swept away in the process. The massive labour surplus of prewar years was changed into an acute labour shortage by the joint demands of munitions production and the armed forces. As a result, no sector of society was left undisturbed by the desperate search for extra manpower to bridge the gap. In prewar years, women of gentle birth were expected to confine their attentions, energies and ambitions to hearth and home, with a modicum of charitable work for the sake of social decency. The war demanded extensive participation by women in the formal labour market, to release men for other duties. Manpower shortages offered the chance of work to the old and partially incapacitated, who had previously struggled to subsist on the fringes of the labour market. At the other end of the social scale, the power and influence of the landed classes dwindled as that of businessmen and financiers rose. In a period of acute social upheaval, skirts grew shorter, beer weaker, gold coin was replaced by paper notes, civil aviation was born and the horse was rendered obsolescent by the spread of motorized transport. Social, economic, technological and scientific change – all stimulated by the war – made a permanent impact on British life and British society.

We might assume that a population at war is a population under pressure, suffering privations in food, clothing and other basic necessities as national resources are poured into the conflict. But, as Peter Dewey shows in Chapter 4, consumption fell by only 20 per cent (of which 7 per cent was accounted for by a reduction in expenditure on alcohol) and for most people the First World War was a period of improvement in Britain, especially for those who had suffered the worst poverty in earlier years.[1] The destitution that had seemed endemic in Edwardian times virtually disappeared. It was never to return, not even at the height of the Slump in the early 1930s. At the end of the nineteenth century social investigators had established a poverty line below which life was deemed impossible. Research in several major British cities found that a tenth of the working class population was in poverty and around a third was seriously at risk of becoming destitute. Thus a substantial minority had insufficient income to procure basic food and shelter; all things considered, it was a miracle they were able to survive at all. The war years changed all that. In the 1920s new research revealed that the incidence of primary poverty had fallen by more than half and that most of what remained was attributable to the recent rise in unemployment.[2] During the war years fewer people claimed relief from the Poor Law and fewer necessitous schoolchildren required subsidized school meals. The number of destitute generally declined.

At the same time standards of health rose. For those fortunate enough to escape service in the trenches, life expectancy increased.[3] There was less illness caused by digestive disorders, diarrhoea and degenerative diseases – since people were eating a greater variety of food and probably more of it. Infant mortality fell. The 'infant mortality rate' (IMR) – the proportion of babies born who fail to survive to their first birthday – is a useful measurement of general standards of living, for when these are low babies die like flies. They were certainly dying in large numbers at the turn of the century; in major industrial cities the IMR stood at around 200 per 1000 live births. By way of comparison, European rates today range from 8 to 20 per 1000 live births. Matters improved steadily before the First World War, more rapidly still during it. In Wigan, to take an example, the IMR averaged 181 between 1901 and 1903. It was 139 on the eve of war and fell to 119 by the Armistice.[4] In crude terms, the annual rate of improvement in the IMR between 1902 and 1914 stood at 3.5; during the four years of war this rose

1 J. M. Winter, *The Great War and the British People* (London: Macmillan, 1985). Statistics used in this chapter referring to mortality, morbidity, wages and earnings and other measures of social improvement are drawn from this text.

2 A. F. Bowley and M. Hogg, *Has Poverty Diminished?* (London: P.S. King, 1925).

3 Winter, *Great War*, pp. 108–15.

4 Winter, *Great War*, p. 148.

to 5. Of course not all towns were as bad as Wigan. However, it typifies the experience of the poorest areas, where progress was most noticeable. Rising rates of infant survival mark Britain as unique among European countries at this time; elsewhere the fluctuating incidence of baby deaths demonstrates how the war was taking its toll on the health of the civilian population.

In seeking an explanation for this improvement in health, we might be tempted to think that it reflects better access to medical care. There is some evidence which, ostensibly, might be taken to support this hypothesis. For some time, public debate had certainly generated a heightened awareness of the risks posed to the community by poor working-class health. During the Boer War (1899–1902) a high proportion of army volunteers had been rejected as physically unfit for service. This had sparked off a major official inquiry into the problem of physical deterioration which was apparently posing such a threat to industry and empire. The discussion stimulated all sorts of reform proposals – ranging from the sterilization of the unfit to a wholesale attack on urban poverty. The First World War saw concern for infant and maternal welfare rise to prominence once again, not least because the birth rate was falling swiftly and the slaughter in the trenches was prompting a new respect for the value of human life. 'If we had been more careful for the last fifty years to prevent the unheeded wastage of human life,' a *Daily Telegraph* leader ran in May 1917, 'we should have had at least half a million more men available for the defence of the country.' Not all attitudes were quite so instrumental. In July 1917, on the eve of Passchendaele, the Bishop of London pointed out in public that during 1915 an average of nine British soldiers – and twelve British babies – had died every hour throughout the year.[5] Such statements were all grist to the reformers' mill. Training for midwives was extended, the numbers of health visitors expanded, Exchequer grants and charitable donations made available for the extension of help to mothers and their babies. Quite how effective these measures were, however, is open to question.

Official concern was not confined to the pregnant and parturating. With labour in such short supply, the health – and thus the potential productivity – of all munition workers became an important component in the war effort. New techniques in scientific management were imported from the United States which effectively

5 Both quotations cited in Winter, *Great War*, p. 193.

improved working conditions.[6] By the end of the war subsidized factory canteens were catering for over one million munition workers every day. Working class consumption of alcohol – which had long alarmed Victorian philanthropists – assumed a new significance as a threat to factory output. Lloyd George, anxious to cause a political stir, claimed it was a major obstacle to the successful prosecution of the war. As a result, new restrictions were imposed on pub licensing hours which are with us to this day. The alcohol content of beer was reduced, and a high tax was placed on spirits which effectively limited their consumption. The drive to maintain output also led the government to try to curb the rising cost of living in order to prevent strikes that would disrupt production. In 1915 rents were officially controlled – ostensibly an important contribution to general welfare as virtually all workers' households were dependent on rented accommodation at this time. Aside from housing, government started subsidizing food prices and introduced a limited scheme of rationing in the course of 1917.

Official action of this kind may have improved health and reduced poverty. However, the fact that new initiatives were taken does not mean that they were instantly effective. In terms of infant welfare at least, social reforms were introduced far too late to explain wartime improvements. The new midwives training scheme was initiated in 1916 and cannot have had any impact before the end of the war. The compulsory provision of maternal and infant welfare centres was introduced only in 1918. Even where facilities already existed, they were limited and the numbers of mothers attending them were very low. More significantly, civilian access to a doctor was made more difficult, not easier, by wartime conditions. The army had an insatiable appetite for qualified medical personnel, and this meant overall numbers of civilian general practitioners dwindled as the war progressed. In major centres of munitions production, matters were even worse as the population was swollen by the influx of a newly expanded workforce. In Birmingham, Coventry, Nottingham, Hull and Newcastle, there were more than 4,000 people for every GP by January 1918; in Glasgow this figure was nearer 5,000. In 1913 the ratio of people to doctors had stood at roughly 2,500 to one – with considerable regional variation. Of the 25,000 doctors, some 14,000 were eventually recruited into the armed services. Again,

6 N. Whiteside, 'Industrial welfare and labour regulation in Britain at the time of the First World War', *International Review of Social History*, vol. 25, no. 3 (1980) pp. 307–331.

Table 5.1   Cost of living and movements in weekly wages among some groups of workers, 1914–1918 (1914 = 100)

Date	Cost of living	Wages all workers	Bricklayers (8 towns)	Bricklayers' labourers (7 towns)	Engineering fitters and turners	Engineering labourers	Shipbuilding platers	Iron and steel: South Wales
1914	100	100	100	100	100	100	100	100
1915	123	111	102	104	110	n.a.	n.a.	102
1916	146	121	109	115	111	n.a.	n.a.	133
1917	176	155	122	134	134	154	169	148
1918	203	195	157	184	173	213	193	159

Date	Coalminers (N.Yorks and Durham) (Earnings)	Compositors (8 Towns)	Railwaymen	Agricultural workers	Cotton workers (Earnings)	Trade Board rates (Men)	Trade board rates (Women)	Dock labourers
1914	100	100	100	100	100	100	100	100
1915	112	100	110	112	103	100	100	111
1916	133	105	120	140	107	100	400	130
1917	158	120	155	189	119	125	135	150
1918	189	156	195	226	157	135	157	193

Source: J.M. Winter, The Great War and the British People (London: Macmillan, 1985), p. 233.

to put this in perspective, there are between 500 and 800 people per doctor in Europe in the 1980s.[7] It appears unlikely that wartime improvements in health can be attributed to the extension of medical services.

Official attempts to combat inflation also met with limited success. Prices rose steadily throughout the war (Table 5.1). Official attempts to regulate the cost of food relied far too long on bureaucratic pleas for voluntary restraint; compulsory rationing had little effect until the last year of the war. Hence, while medical evidence indicates that nutrition improved, this was not simply the result of effective state regulation.

Nor were rent controls an overwhelming success. Lacking any official means of administration, their improvement fell to local labour organizations who acted on behalf of tenants. The lay magistracy, many of whom were landlords themselves, proved less than totally sympathetic. Initially at least, there was no penalty for contravening the Rent Restriction Act of 1915. As a result, it was broken continually. The rising cost of housing remained a thorn in the flesh of working people, especially in centres of munitions production where accommodation was very limited. Indeed, the Rent Restriction Act did nothing to alleviate the problem of overcrowding, which became increasingly serious. Shortages of building material and labour meant very few houses were built during the war, thus exacerbating the existing housing problem inherited from prewar years. In major munition centres the situation was made worse by the immigration of new workers. In Barrow-in-Furness, home of Vickers munition works, the population grew by 10,000 in two years. By 1917 there was an official average of 6.5 persons per house in the town.[8] Such levels of overcrowding helped raise the incidence of tuberculosis (TB), one of the major diseases which showed no sign of declining during the war.

Housing in general – and the housing of munitions workers in particular – was a controversial problem from which government could not extricate itself. If rents went up, workers would demand higher wages, thus raising the cost of munitions production and with it the cost of the war. If rents were controlled landlords' profits would vanish, property would remain in poor repair, housing would lose its appeal for the private investor and the construction of new stock

7 Winter, *Great War*, pp. 179 and 186.
8 D. Englander, *Landlord and Tenant* (Oxford: Oxford University Press, 1983) pp. 236 and 243. For a thorough account of the housing question during the war, see chs. 10–12.

would cease. In the event, official controls on rents had precisely those consequences. By the time of the Armistice, the market was so depressed that a state-subsidized house building programme was the only way to relieve the chronic shortages and to prevent a further rise in the incidence of unrest these had already provoked. The Housing Act of 1919 was an emergency measure designed to alleviate a temporary imbalance between supply and demand for housing caused by the war. State intervention, however, proved anything but temporary. During the next decade governments of various political complexions struggled to subsidize house building in the public and private sectors in order to raise the quantity of housing available at rents working people could afford. Any beneficial effects of state action in this area on standards of living, however, lay far in the future.

Social improvement, therefore, does not appear to have sprung from government intervention in the supply of housing, food or medical resources. The main reasons why health standards rose and the incidence of poverty declined are found elsewhere – principally in rising household earnings. Nothing cures poverty like more money. The state certainly played its part here by subsidizing those who, thanks to the war, had lost their main source of income. The most obvious beneficiaries were the families of men recruited into the armed forces. After the war, separation allowances, widows' pensions and payments to disabled ex-servicemen were costing the government over £92 million a year. Of course, state welfare payments – in the form of old age pensions and national insurance – had been introduced before the war. However, payments were low and their impact on poverty therefore limited. Indeed, in 1920 war pensions were costing more than twice the sum of old age pensions and official unemployment benefits combined. Government also accepted responsibility for those whose earnings and employment were disrupted by the war. The wages of cotton operatives, many of whom were on short-time working owing to the war, were 'made up' under a scheme created by government for the industry. After the Armistice, the state's Out of Work Donation scheme provided generous rates of relief for both unemployed civilians and ex-servicemen seeking new jobs. This set a precedent for state funded 'doles' which persisted throughout the interwar period. In this way, government's responsibilities in the field of income maintenance were extended – and extended permanently – by the war.

Although cash benefits and pensions play some part in explaining the disappearance of poverty, the main causes are to be found in the labour market – chiefly in the growth of employment and in rising levels of take-home pay. The expansion of the war economy, together with the heavy demands of the armed services, bit deep into manpower resources and increased demand for female and juvenile labour . Thus, the number of wage earners in working class households grew. Irregular and casual employment, endemic in many Edwardian cities, virtually disappeared. Young people – as young as 12–14 years old – found they could now command wages undreamed of before the war and their increasing independence led to much speculation about lost parental discipline and the growth of. juvenile delinquency Women also entered the labour market in large numbers, their formal employment increasing by almost a million during the war. At the same time the numbers of domestic servants fell by 400,000, probably because better pay and conditions were easily obtainable elsewhere. The use of female workers expanded chiefly in munitions (by 700,000), in transport (by 100,000) and in banking, finance, commerce and public administration (by 400,000). Women and girls were also to be found in growing numbers in other areas – such as agriculture and retailing – as well as winning entry to the armed services themselves. And, of course, these figures do not include the legions of voluntary workers running everything from camp canteens to sewing classes for expectant mothers, who came forward to 'do their bit' for the war.

Not all gains in women's formal employment proved permanent. The introduction of women into engineering, for example, was negotiated with the trade union (the Amalgamated Society of Engineers) as an emergency measure which would end when hostilities ceased. Throughout the war, however, skilled engineers viewed the new arrivals with some foreboding. In order to expand production, tasks hitherto reserved for skilled men were redesigned into a series of semi-skilled or unskilled jobs, capable of being performed by labour with little or no experience or training. This process was called 'dilution', and the 'dilutees' were mostly female . The original object of the exercise was to conserve precious reserves of skilled men who were to be directed to essential tasks – including the supervision of these new industrial recruits. The scheme, however, provoked resentment. If work could be performed by unskilled labour during the war, there was no incentive for employers to restore prewar practices after the Armistice. Strikes on the Clyde in 1916 centred on precisely this issue. Further trouble broke out when dilution, initially confined to government war contracts, was extended to private work in 1917. By this time many were complaining that dilution was not being used to release skilled men for essential war work but to substitute women for men who were being sent as cannon fodder to the trenches. In order to restore industrial peace both government and engineering employers had little hesitation in dispensing with women's services at the end of the war.

Similar trends were also visible elsewhere. Women recruited to the wartime civil service were often offered only temporary contracts; when peace returned, overt preference was given to ex-servicemen in appointments to established posts. In both government service and teaching, formal marriage bars were introduced after the war to guarantee that women left work permanently once they had secured an alternative means of support. As unemployment rose in 1921, so employment exchanges put increased pressure on women to return to domestic service, to make good the 'servant shortage' which was causing such difficulties in the middle and upper echelons of society and which was also seen as a product of the war. For women in general and married women in particular, the importance of their domestic role was reasserted. The only permanent gain in terms of women's job opportunities lay in the sphere of secretarial services and in the expansion of department stores at the expense of the corner shop, which increased women's employment in retailing. However, in both cases, formal and informal marriage bars existed and these advances in work opportunities therefore benefited girls more than women.

None of this should detract from the very real gains made by women during the war itself.Munitions work, in particular, paid far higher wages than the jobs available to women before the war had ever done. Employers, desperate to raise productivity, used piece rates and war bonus payments to encourage extra effort from their labour force. In general, such systems benefited unskilled workers more than the skilled; the latter's wages, based on time rates, tended to lag behind. Hence the greatest benefits of higher earnings went to the lowest paid, helping eliminate poverty while reducing the wage differentials between skilled and unskilled workers. This provoked resentment and bitterness. Skilled men were less successful in keeping up with inflation; in at least one instance reports were made of qualified engineers taking on unskilled work because this actually increased their take-home pay. Although wages roughly doubled during the war, workers directly involved in the war economy benefited more than those outside it. Those in building, textiles or printing, for example, did less well (Table 5.1). In very general terms, wartime inflation inflicted most damage on the livelihoods of craftsmen and skilled workers; it also hurt all groups on fixed incomes – notably landlords and landowners heavily reliant on rents. The cost of the conflict did not fall on the shoulders of the poorest in the community.

Rising wages were not, however, the result of effective state regulation – or the extension of industrial largesse. On the contrary, government was the chief customer of the munitions factories and thus had a vested interest in keeping wages down. The 1915 Treasury Agreement negotiated by Lloyd George with the TUC took steps to prevent workers taking advantage of relatively full employment, by outlawing strikes and referring all industrial disputes to official arbitration. During its first two years, the system worked, after a fashion. There were strikes - notably on the Clyde against dilution in 1916 – but wages rose by only 10 per cent or so per year. However, in the last two years of the war matters got out of hand; the number of disputes escalated and wages went up annually by 30 or 40 per cent. A major inquiry in 1917 into the causes of unrest laid bare the roots of working class discontent. The question of manpower controls aside, overcrowding, food prices and high rents all proved to be common complaints. Resentment was made all the more bitter by the feeling that workers were suffering disproportionately as a result of the war. Their mobility was constrained, their wages failed to keep pace with rising prices, while their employers were making fat profits at public expense, profits in which workers could claim no share.[9] Wartime profiteering was indeed widespread, notably in coalmining and shipbuilding; the widespread demand for the 'conscription of wealth' received vociferous support within the Labour movement.[10]

Although strikes were illegal in theory, there was little the government could do when faced with mass industrial action in a key sector of the war economy. Emergency powers allowed the prosecution and imprisonment of offenders; however, such action – even if physically possible – was liable to provoke further unrest and thus threaten further disruption of essential supplies. As early as July 1915 when 200,000 coalminers in south Wales went on strike, Lloyd George concluded that tactical concessions were sometimes the only answer, to the intense irritation of his civil servants who favoured a tougher approach.[11] Giving the miners higher wages achieved immediate peace but undermined the authority of the official wage

9 *Reports of the Enquiry into Industrial Unrest*, *P.P.* 1917–18, Cd 8662–9, 8696, xv.

10 R. Harrison, 'The War Emergency Workers' National Committee' in A. Briggs and J. Saville (eds), *Essays in Labour History 1886–1923* (London: Macmillan, 1971) pp. 211–60.

11 J. Harris, *William Beveridge* (Oxford: Oxford University Press, 1977), pp. 216–27.

arbitration system, whose award had provoked strike action in the first place. Not all stoppages guaranteed victory to the workers; unrest on the Clyde in 1916 met with a far less conciliatory response. Historians interested in wartime unrest have tended to focus on the strikes caused by dilution and manpower controls.[12] Although these were often larger and more dramatic, the overwhelming majority of stoppages concerned questions of pay and working conditions.[13] As unrest threatened to disrupt the production of munitions, public officials and employers alike proved generally willing to offer additional financial incentives in that sector, which explains why earnings rose faster there than elsewhere. What all this means is that rising wage-levels in the latter years of the war were the result of direct action taken by the workers themselves – or the threat of it. Similarly, the Rent Restriction Act of 1915 was also a direct response to working class unrest, particularly apparent in the rent strikes in London, Birmingham and Glasgow during 1915. Similar direct action on rents also convinced the government that controls must be continued at the end of the war.[14] Improved living standards were thus no mere fortuitous consequence of the war but were won through the rising influence of organized labour in both political and industrial sectors.

Certainly by 1917 official efforts to prevent wage escalation lay in ruins. The Committee on Production (which was charged with official arbitration) had wanted to create a central hierarchy of national wage agreements adjusted periodically in accordance with the cost of living. As a result, formal recognition of trade unions spread and regional – even national – systems of wage bargaining were established in industries previously unorganized. In munitions, on the other hand, the objective proved to be a pipe dream. Early in the war, labour policy had been fairly coherent – when Lloyd George did not intervene unilaterally to impose his own solutions on industrial discontents. As the conflict progressed, the number of government departments concerned with the process of production – and thus with industrial relations – expanded accordingly. The pro-

12 e.g. J. Hinton, *The First Shop Stewards Movement* (London: Allen & Unwin, 1973); also J. Hinton, 'The Clyde Workers' Committee and the dilution struggle', in Briggs and Saville, *Essays in Labour History*, pp. 152–85.
13 A. Reid, 'Dilution, trade unionism and the state in Britain during the First World War', in S. Tolliday and J. Zeitlin (eds), *Shop Floor Bargaining and the State* (Cambridge: Cambridge University Press, 1985) pp. 46–74.
14 Englander, *Landlord and Tenant*, pp. 205–31 and 267.

liferation of bureaucracy increased the likelihood that government's right hand rarely knew, or cared, what its left hand was doing. Production departments – individually concerned with coal or shipping, naval supply or army munitions – proved very reluctant to refer industrial disputes in their sector to the lengthy process of official arbitration. Instead, they encouraged employers to buy their way out of trouble. Such practices restored the importance of workshop bargaining and increased the powers of shop stewards (who might, or might not, be union appointees). As a result, a merry-go-round of disputes and settlements developed, with an award in one workshop sparking off demands for equal treatment elsewhere. Hence by the end of the war some groups of workers were markedly better off than others – even in the same industry. The short boom in the immediate aftermath of the conflict saw the continuation of wage disputes as the less fortunate tried to catch up, as the strikes by the railwaymen, the police and the Lancashire cotton workers in 1919 bear witness. The extension of collective bargaining as well as this growth of direct action were reflected in the expansion of trade union organization, notably among unskilled workers. Membership grew from 4 million at the start of the war to 6 million at the time of the Armistice, peaking at 8.3 million in 1920 – almost half of the total working population.[15]

Although the Cabinet, disturbed by the example of the Russian revolutions, grew alarmed at the spread of industrial militancy, the British labour movement betrayed little revolutionary intent. This might perhaps be explained by the haphazard mixture of concession and coercion with which wartime administration handled working-class discontents. But this is not to argue that the war had no effect on social attitudes or political behaviour. By 1922 Seebohm Rowntree could note how working people 'now claim as a right a better maintenance than they would once have begged as a privilege'.[16] The war had shown how requests for redress of grievances voiced through the proper channels were nowhere near as effective as open demands backed by the threat of direct action. The extension of the franchise in 1918 and the growth of trade union membership offered the poorer sections of the working population the chance to preserve the very real gains they had made during the war. Britain's industrial workforce emerged from the war more homoge-

15 G. R. Askwith, *Industrial Problems and Disputes* (New York: Harper & Row, 1974) pp. 414–46.
16 Cited in W. G. Runciman, *Relative Deprivation and Social Justice* (London: Routledge & Kegan Paul, 1966) p. 56.

nous, less poverty stricken and more organized than it had been in 1914.

It also formed a smaller component of British society as a whole. The number of 'white collar' salaried employees rose by over a million between 1911 and 1921, from 12 to 22 per cent of the working population. The expansion of business and financial institutions produced a new host of office workers at one end of the social scale while at the same time changing the composition of social and political elites at the other. The old upper classes whose wealth was based on property and land did not do well out of the war. Rent controls undermined land values. Exorbitant death duties forced the sale of major estates at knockdown prices in the aftermath of the war. The sons of the landed classes bore a disproportionate toll of war fatalities, frequently depriving old estates of the sort of energetic management necessary if they were to remain viable in depressed agricultural conditions. Their place at the summit of society was taken over by commercial and business leaders, frequently men whose fortunes had been founded during the war and who had been drawn into politics by Lloyd George's belief in the efficacy of business enterprise in the execution of public affairs. Acquiring the titles and honours to give credit to their new-found status, they merged imperceptibly into the traditional structure of British society. In this way, the war changed the composition of social classes without transforming the relationship between them.

This longer term outcome was not immediately obvious. For a short period at the end of the war, British social and political life was dominated by two powerful and opposing forces. On the one hand, industrial employers and the business world wished to shrug off government controls and to return to prewar days of plentiful and cheap labour, of unfettered managerial prerogative and social privilege. On the other hand, the newly extended labour organizations – ranging from local trades councils and tenants' associations to national trade unions and the Labour Party itself – were fighting to consolidate and extend wartime gains. The crisis proved transitory. In the short term, substantial concessions were made to labour in order to preserve stability. In the longer term, rising unemployment in the 1920s undermined labour militancy and did much to restore more traditional forms of order and industrial discipline. However, the established social protocol and traditional hierarchies of Edwardian Britain did not re-emerge. Nor did the chronic working class poverty and poor health of the prewar years. In the First World War we find the roots of a new social and political order, arguably less rigid, less paternalist and less deferential than the one which had preceded it.

6

The British Army, 1914–18: The Illusion of Change

IAN BECKETT

Many students are now familiar with Professor Arthur Marwick's 'four-tier model' with respect to the impact of a 'total' war such as that fought between 1914 and 1918. It is assumed that such a conflict will bring destruction and disruption on an unprecedented scale and that the institutions of a state and its society will be so tested by the experience that they might conceivably collapse altogether. There will be increased participation in the war effort at all levels of society, and individuals as well as society as a whole will undergo a 'colossal psychological experience'.[1] The cumulative effect will be real and enduring social change. To be fair to Marwick, the model was presented merely as a 'rough tool', which could be adopted or rejected at will, but it is undeniable that the Marwickian interpretation of war as a determinant of change has had a profound impact on the historiography of war over the past decade. However, it is equally clear that the link between war and change, on occasions, has been pushed too far. It is the purpose of this essay, therefore, to examine the impact of the First World War upon one particular institution of state in order to assess how far such a total conflict did represent an agent of change. The chosen institution is the British army.

Superficially, the army appears to fit the Marwickian model exceptionally well. In August 1914 there were 733,514 officers and men serving in the regular army, the part-time Territorial Force and other reserve formations, of which only 247,432 were serving in the regular army itself. But in the course of the next four years a further 4,907,902 men enlisted in the army and the Territorials – a figure equivalent to 22.11 per cent of the entire male population of the

---

1 Arthur Marwick, *War and Social Change in the Twentieth Century* (London: Macmillan, 1974), pp. 11–14.

United Kingdom.[2] In all, therefore, a total of 5,704,416 men served in the British army between August 1914 and November 1918 (Table 6.1), representing a sevenfold increase over the maximum size of the army and reserves when the war began. Moreover, while Britain had enjoyed a voluntary system of enlistment before the war, demands for manpower at the front resulted in the progressive extension of conscription from January 1916 onwards. Such massive expansion, involving the reintroduction of a form of military service shunned for over a century, challenged the social structure of the army as it had existed before the war. Comparatively few had served in the armed forces before 1914, but now an approximation of a Continental-style 'nation in arms' brought millions of men into contact with an institution in which they would never have served under normal conditions.

That 2,471,142 of those who did serve in the army during the war became casualties between August 1914 and September 1919 – killed, wounded, missing or made prisoner – is evidence enough both of the destructiveness and the likely psychological effect of the war.[3] Indeed, in 1980 there were still 27,000 men alive in Britain who were receiving disability pensions as a result of injuries sustained during the First World War.[4] Similarly, the popular perception of the war is still rooted firmly in the particular horrors of the Western Front and the literature of disillusionment associated with Wilfred Owen, Robert Graves and Siegfried Sassoon. It is an image which seems for ever to stand as a monument to the trauma of the war.

Yet much of that popular perception is mythology and the student should not assume either that Owen or Graves was representative of the millions who served in the army during the war, or that the change wrought in the army as an institution through expansion necessarily persisted once wartime servicemen had been demobilized. In these respects, it is worth examining in detail three particular aspects of the army's experience. First, how far those who enlisted in the wartime army differed from those who had done so before the war. Second, what was the impact of service life and of war upon those who enlisted. Third, how far did the army itself change as a result of its wartime expansion.

2 *Statistics of the Military Effort of the British Empire during the Great War* (London: HMSO, 1922), pp.30, 156–9, 363–4.

3 *General Annual Returns of the British Army for the period from 1 October 1913 to 30 September 1919*, *P.P.* 1920, Cmd. 1193, xv.

4 Lyn Macdonald, *The Roses of No Man's Land* (London: Michael Joseph, 1980), pp. 217–19, 293–304.

Table   6.1   *Enlistments in the regular army
and Territorial Force, 1914–18*

Month	Total
August 1914	298,923
September	462,901
October	136,811
November	169,862
December	117,860
January 1915	156,290
February	87,896
March	113,907
April	119,087
May	135,263
June	114,679
July	95,413
August	95,980
September	71,617
October	113,285
November	121,793
December	55,152
Total	2,446,719
January 1916 to November 1918	2,504,183
August 1914 to November 1918	4,970,902
Strength of British army, Territorials and Reserves, August 1914	733,514
Total serving in British army, 1914–18	5,704,416

Source: *Statistics of the Military Effort of the British Empire during the Great War* (London: HMSO, 1922) p. 364.

The prewar regular army in Britain had changed in some respects from that of Victoria's reign, notably in advances in its training and tactics; but the improvement in its professionalism, a result of lessons absorbed in the South African war , had been accomplished without the army becoming any more representative of society as a whole. Officers were still drawn largely from traditional elites, and rank reflected a close correlation with the land, although it should be emphasized that the landed interest was an open group and that those who had acquired wealth from commerce or industry had used the army frequently as an entrée to society. In any case, the majority of candidates for commission were the products of the public schools.

At the other extreme, the army's rank and file was still largely dependent upon the lowest classes of society. Overwhelmingly English in nationality, the army was also largely urban in origin. Unskilled labourers provided the largest single category of recruit and, although the army did not keep statistics of the numbers who were unemployed, a report on the health of the army in 1909 revealed that over 90 per cent of those presenting themselves for medical inspection as recruits were without employment.[5] In the following year, 55 per cent of all who offered themselves were rejected on medical or other grounds, the poor health and physique of would-be recruits reflecting a level of poverty and malnutrition in urban society which would now be associated with the Third World. In short, the burden of military service fell unequally in society and represented what Field Marshal Lord Nicholson had once called the 'compulsion of destitution'.[6] Behind the regulars stood the Special Reserve and the Territorial Force, both established in 1908 as replacements respectively for the militia and the yeomanry and volunteers. The Special Reserve, like the militia before it, was no more than a draft-finding body for the army which drew precisely upon the same pool of recruits. Similarly, although the Territorials embraced elements of the middle classes, the force as a whole was dependent upon the working class for its recruits, albeit skilled manual workers in receipt of regular wages rather than the casually employed found in the ranks of the army.

It might be expected, therefore, that the expansion that took place between 1914 and 1918 should result in new sources of manpower being tapped and in the burden of military service becoming more equitably distributed between social groups. In fact research, both into the pattern of voluntary enlistment in 1914 and 1915 and the way in which conscription was applied after 1916, suggests that this did not happen.

In terms of voluntary enlistment, the traditional interpretation has been one of an overwhelming patriotic rush to enlist upon the outbreak of war, with recruiting offices across Europe besieged by young men engaged, like so many lemmings, in a collective rendezvous with death. In Britain, although 15 per cent of all wartime enlistments took place in the first two months of the war, the 'rush to the colours' was not immediate and has been dated almost precisely to the period between 25 August and 9 September 1914, after which the same degree of enthusiasm never recurred. The pro-

5 *Report on the Health of the Army for the year 1909*, *P.P.* 1911, Cmd 5477, xlvii.
6 Public Record Office, WO 105/41, Nicholson to Roberts, 10 November 1906.

cess of enlistment was complex, with wide regional and local variations in response. Of course, patriotism played its part, and the British public had been conditioned in advance to meet the challenge of war through the militarization of schools and youth organizations, through the influence of the press and popular literature, even through the industrial militancy of the Edwardian age. But the response to the appeals to enlist was also determined by many other factors. One was certainly family situation, and there is a body of evidence to suggest that inefficiency by the War Office in paying out adequate separation allowances discouraged many married men from enlisting, while others with dependants who did so took time to put their domestic affairs in order before they volunteered. Equally, there were those who were only too glad to escape family or, indeed, the humdrum routine of civilian life.

Detailed studies have now shown a particular link between employment and enlistment in August and September 1914. Numbers on labour-exchange registers had increased by over 80,000 from mid-July figures by 14 August alone, and it is possible that as many as 480,000 men lost their jobs by the end of August 1914. Many others were placed on half time in the prevailing economic uncertainty at the outbreak of war. In Birmingham, 78 per cent of all recruits in August came from the same classes who had supplied recruits for the regular army in peacetime, the majority from less secure employment that experienced traditional seasonal labour fluctuations in summer. In Bristol, 10 per cent of the labour force had been laid off in July and a further 26 per cent placed on short time: nine out of every ten men laid off in the city enlisted. Similarly, in Leeds enlistment reduced the contraction of employment from 10.25 per cent in August to 1.5 per cent in September. More circumstantially, the Dundee journalist William Lintorn Andrews was pushed to the back of a recruiting queue in August by a man insisting that Andrews 'make way for us lads wi'out jobs'.[7] Significantly, enlistment dropped away rapidly as large government contracts were placed in the autumn for clothing, boots, munitions and other essentials.

Within industry, wage rates as such do not appear to have been a major factor in determining the rate of enlistment but, as Peter Dewey has demonstrated, the response from industry did reflect the actual age-structure of the labour force in differing sectors.[8] Not unnaturally, there was a tendency for younger men to enlist rather

7 W. L. Andrews, *Haunting Years* (London: Hutchinson, n.d.), p. 11.
8 P. E. Dewey, 'Military recruiting and the British labour force during the First World War', *Historical Journal*, vol. 27, no. 1 (1984), pp. 199–224.

than older men and, for example, it so happened that the agricultural labour force was older on average than that in the building trade. Thus, it might be expected that more would enlist from the building trade than from agriculture and such proved the case. From the beginning, too, there was a degree of protection for key workers from the pressures to enlist. Such protection extended to railway workers and also to key Admiralty workers, who were 'badged' well before December 1914.

Then again, enlistment was affected by the way in which a War Office swamped by the demands made on its recruiting system – a clear example of an institution failing the challenge of war – attempted to control the flow of recruits by introducing deferred enlistment and by lowering or raising age limits and physical requirements to an extent that many assumed that their services were not actually required. Others enlisted under the influence of what has been termed 'social inheritance', joining because their friends had done so. The most obvious manifestation of the latter was the success of the 'Pals' battalions of which 115 were raised including such units as the 'Stockbrokers' Battalion' (10th Royal Fusiliers), the 'Hull Commercials' (10th East Yorkshire Regiment), the 'Accrington Pals' (11th East Lancashire Regiment) and the 'Glasgow Corporation Tramways Battalion' (15th Highland Light Infantry). Some reasons why men enlisted defy any categorization. Sidney Rogerson, for example, who served in the 2nd West Yorkshire Regiment, describes how his soldier servant had enlisted in an alcoholic haze after seeing a friend off to the front, never remembered 'taking the shilling, and "when the sergeant comes and claimed" him next morning he was as surprised as his wife was annoyed'.[9]

Whatever the reasons for enlistment, the effect of what occurred in August and September 1914 was that certain groups were far more willing to enlist than others. There was a correction on what might be termed a 'national' basis (Table 6.2) in that Wales and Scotland increased the proportion of their males under arms to a level which largely matched that of England. But, seen from the perspective of sectoral distribution of occupation (Table 6.3), some groups bore a disproportionately high share of the military effort. By February 1916, for example, the sampling surveys of the Board of Trade indicated that, whereas over 40 per cent of those engaged in the professions, entertainment, finance and commerce had enlisted, less than 30 per cent of those in industry as a whole, agriculture or transport had done so. As Jay Winter has remarked, 'men engaged

9 Sidney Rogerson, *Twelve Days* (London: Arthur Barker, 1933), p.40.

Table 6.2   *Enlistments in the United Kingdom, 1914–18*

	England	Wales	Scotland	Ireland
Voluntary Enlistments to Dec. 1915	2,092,242	145,255	320,589	117,063
Proportion of males aged 15–49 enlisted to Dec. 1915	24.2		26.9	10.7
Enlistments after Jan. 1916	1,913,916	127,669	237,029	17,139
Proportion of males aged 15–49 enlisted after Jan. 1916	22.1		14.6	1.6
Total enlistments 1914–18	4,006,158	272,924	557,618	134,202
Proportion of males aged 15–49 enlisted 1914–18	46.2		41.4	12.3
Proportion of all males enlisted 1914–18	24.0	21.5	23.7	6.1
Proportion of regular army 1913	78.6	1.4	7.6	9.1

Source: *Statistics of the Military Effort of the British Empire* (London: HMSO, 1922); J. M. Winter, 'Britain's lost generation of the First World War', *Population Studies*, vol. 31, no. 3 (1977), p. 451; *General Annual Report of the British Army for the Year ending 30 September 1913*, *P.P.* 1914, Cmd 725.

in commercial or distributive trades were in uniform and at risk for longer periods and in relatively larger numbers than were industrial workers, transport workers or agricultural workers'.[10]

Nor was it the case that the introduction of conscription equal-

10 J. M. Winter, 'Britain's lost generation of the First World War', *Population Studies*, vol. 31, no. 3 (1977), pp. 449–66.

ized the discrepancies. There were leniently applied exemptions, particularly for key occupational groups such as agricultural workers, transport workers, miners and the public services (Table 6.4). Moreover, the sheer physical unfitness of many working class men ensured that the burden remained unequal to the end: over a million men out of the 2.5 million examined by Ministry of National Service medical boards in the last year of the war were rejected . In effect, although far more of a 'nation in arms' than ever before, the army was still just as unrepresentative of society as a whole during the war as it had been in peacetime. In those circumstances, the impact of war casualties was dysgenic since the upper and middle classes of society did suffer proportionately heavier losses and, in this sense, there was a very large element of truth in the contemporary idea of a 'lost generation'.

Table 6.3   *Enlistment by industrial sector,*
            August 1914–February 1916

Occupation	Men employed July 1914 ('000)	Men who enlisted ('000)	Percentage of prewar labour force volunteering
Industry	6,165	1,743	28.3
(Mines and quarries)	(1,266)	(313)	(24.7)
Agriculture	920	259	28.2
Transport	1,041	233	22.4
Finance and commerce	1,249	501	40.1
Professions	144	60	41.7
Entertainment	177	74	41.8
Central government	311	85	27.3
Local government	477	126	26.4
All occupations	10,484	3,081	29.4

Source: Public Record Office, Reconstruction Papers, 1/832, tabulated in J. M. Winter, 'Britain's lost generation of the First World War', *Population Studies*, vol. 31, no. 3 (1977), p. 454.

Turning to the impact of service life upon those who did serve in the army, there is far less truth in the concept of a 'war generation', a universality of experience linking officers and men in a common community of spirit bred in the trenches. It is a concept one associates with the work of Robert Graves or Siegfried Sassoon. Another example is the novelist and later popular broad-

Table 6.4   *Enlistment by occupational sector (4.1 repeated)*

	July 1916	July 1918
Commerce	41	63
Manufacturing	30	45
Public service	27	39
Transport	23	38
Agriculture	22	35

Source: Board of Trade, *Reports on the State of Employment*, 1916, 1918, tabulated in P. E. Dewey, 'Military recruiting and the British labour force during the First World War', *Historical Journal*, vol. 27, no. 1 (1984), p. 205.

caster, Christopher Stone, whose sense of social responsibility was awakened by the war.[11] However, there are distinct dangers in accepting such men as in any way representative of wartime soldiers as a whole. Not all who served in the British army were as well educated as these literary critics, whose disillusionment in a postwar world reflected the contrast between the romantic naïveté with which they had gone to war and the realities of a brutal, impersonal and industrialized conflict. The development of ex-servicemen's associations in Britain, with more radical elements rapidly neutralized through the emergence of an all-embracing British Legion in 1921, suggests that many wartime soldiers were far more concerned with the prospects for civil resettlement than with the expression of any shared experience in the army. Some veterans' groups were particularly antagonistic towards the army. It can be equally noted that the only really serious disciplinary problems in the British army came not during the war itself but after it, when a series of disturbances in England, France and elsewhere were motivated primarily by a demand for demobilization.

Throughout the war, divisions within the army were profound. The greatest gulf was between officer and man. Although officers were promoted increasingly from the ranks, their separate status and privilege were marked in innumerable ways: by better rations, better dugouts, greater periods of leave, greater freedom of movement, even separate cinemas and brothels. Of course, regimental officers shared the dangers of the front line with their men, played games

11 On Stone, see G. D. Sheffield, 'The effect of war service on the 2nd Battalion, Royal Fusiliers (Kensingtons), 1914–1918 with special reference to morale, discipline and the officer/man relationship', Unpublished MA thesis, Leeds University, 1984 fos 82–97.

with them and cared for them, but one needs only to sample the wealth of contemporary other-ranks' trench newspapers[12] to comprehend that the sharing of activities was not recognized by the rank and file as amounting to a 'celebration of community' as some have implied. There were also other divisions. That between front and rear and that between 'staff' and regimental officers figured no more and no less in the First World War than in any other. At the front itself, there were divisions between the various arms and branches of the army and between specialists such as machine gunners and the ordinary infantry. The last held some groups in particular contempt, such as the trench mortar crews whose activity could bring a 'tit for tat' barrage down upon the infantry from across no man's land, or the Royal Engineers who made such great demands on the infantry for labour when the infantry were supposedly 'at rest'. There were differences between infantry divisions, some being 'holding' formations and others 'assault' divisions. And there were the differences between Regular soldiers, Territorials and the men of the 'New Armies'.

Not surprisingly, the Regular army's divisions, twelve infantry and three mounted divisions, were those committed first to overseas active service. Since Kitchener, who was appointed as Secretary of State for War in August 1914, chose to ignore the existing machinery of Territorial County Associations as a basis for wartime expansion, two-thirds of those who enlisted between August 1914 and December 1915 joined units of the so-called 'Kitchener' or 'New' Army – in all, thirty New Army infantry divisions were formed. In the mean time, however, many of those formations reaching the Western Front and other theatres in late 1914 and during 1915 were from the twenty-eight infantry and five mounted divisions of the Territorial Force. Understandably, there were rivalries between such formations and especially between Territorials and men of the New Army.

As the war continued, so the distinction between regulars, Territorials and New Army men became blurred as any pretence to draft men from a particular area to a particular unit was sacrificed to the military necessity of ensuring that losses were made good. Indeed, as decisions were made as to the appropriate deployment of available manpower between the army and essential war industries, so reductions and amalgamations were effected in the army. In the spring of 1918, for example, seventeen infantry divisions were either broken

12 John Fuller, 'Industrial entertainment for industrial war: the British army overseas, 1914-1918', paper presented to Cambridge University war studies seminar at Corpus Christi College, 14 March 1984.

up, reconstituted or reduced to cadre prior to reconstitution. But, if units were fed increasingly from the same pool of manpower, there was still a distinction between those who had volunteered in 1914 and 1915 and those who had been conscripted from 1916 onwards. Much is now known of the mechanics of conscription and the particular treatment of conscientious objectors, but little is known as yet of the vast majority of conscripts' experience in the army. The general impression from contemporary accounts is that reinforcements received after 1918 were from the 'bottom of the barrel' – men of progressively declining intelligence, physique and commitment, or mere boys.[13]

The actual welcome afforded new arrivals in a unit could vary widely, and it must be emphasized that the conditioning of men like Graves, Sassoon or Stone depended entirely upon the unit in which they actually served. From case-studies so far undertaken, it is apparent that no one battalion was quite like any other and that generalizing the experience of war is exceptionally difficult. It can be said that individuals who served in the army would all have undergone a process of socialization into military life and its demands. Not least, they would have needed to come to terms with the code of military discipline, although it has been suggested that the subordination and tedium commonplace in British industrial society and the predisposition in popular culture to make light of hardship enabled a majority of wartime servicemen to accommodate their new environment.

Many would certainly have experienced an end to innocence in its widest sense. To give but one example, Charles Cain of the 2/5th Manchesters learned much of what he termed the 'wine, women and song bit' especially when billeted at Stockport during the first winter of the war. Cain recounts how one ex-miner in his battalion had the habit of walking around naked in the billet: 'He called this advertising, but as far as I know it had the opposite effect to what he wanted, for she [the landlady] locked herself in the kitchen and her complaints landed Charlie in the guardroom.'[14] Again, a trooper of the socially prestigious 1/2nd County of London Yeomanry (Westmin-

13 See, for example, Andrews, *Haunting Years*, p.213; 'Rifleman', *Four Years on the Western Front* (London: Odhams, 1922), pp. 152, 332; W. H. A. Groom, *Poor Bloody Infantry* (London: William Kimber, 1976), p. 45.
14 Imperial War Museum, PP/MCR/48, Cain Mss, quoted by Peter Simkins, 'Soldiers and civilians' in I. F. W. Beckett and Keith Simpson (eds), *A Nation in Arms: A Social Study of the British Army in the First World War* (Manchester: Manchester University Press, 1985), pp.165–92.

ster Dragoons), sharing accommodation in a troopship in September 1914 with men of the 1/9th Manchesters, described the latter as 'the commonest lot of men I ever saw' and complained that 'their lack of manners and filthy habits are more than we can stand' .[15] Certainly, many were exposed to colleagues of widely differing social backgrounds and mores, and military service would have broadened horizons and brought an awareness likely to cut across social divisions and the marked parochialism of prewar society.

Men would have experienced, too, what American servicemen in Vietnam would later call 'turbulence' – the constant change of personalities within a unit. Men left because they became casualties from battle or disease; they went on leave or on courses; they left to become commissioned; they were drafted to other units. Thus, most formations steadily lost any real connection with the particular locality or social group from which they might have been raised originally and, in any case, such links were often tenuous from the very beginning. The 9th Devons, for example, had only eighty Devonians in the battalion when raised in 1914 while the London Irish allegedly had only two genuine Irishmen.[16] It was simply not the case that a man would stay with one unit throughout the war. Nor, of course, would a man serve continuously at the front. To give one example, Charles Carrington, who served in the 1/5th Royal Warwicks, recorded that during 1916 he spent 65 days in the front line, 36 days in close support to the front line, 120 days in reserve, 73 days at rest behind the lines and the remaining 72 days variously on leave, sick, travelling or attending courses.[17] Thus, there was a difference between a unit's total strength on paper, its ration strength in reality, and its trench strength.

Similarly, it must be recognized that conditions of service varied enormously from front to front. The war was not confined to France and Flanders, and British troops served throughout the world (Table 6.5). Even on the Western Front, experience varied from sector to sector. Some areas were acknowledged as 'active' and others as 'quiet', where some kind of informal truce existed between the opposing front lines. In the case of the 56th (1st London) Division, its wartime service in France and Flanders comprised 330 days at

15 Imperial War Museum, P430, Politzer Mss, unidentified letter from RMS *Aragon*, 14 September 1914.
16 C. T. Atkinson, *The Devonshire Regiment,1914-1918* (Exeter: Eland, 1926), pp. 54-5; Patrick MacGill, *The Amateur Army* (London: Herbert Jenkins, 1915), p. 15.
17 Charles Edmonds [sc. Carrington], *A Subaltern's War* (London: Peter Davies, 1929), p. 120.

Table 6.5   *Summary of war casualties in the British army,*
by theatre, 4 August 1914 to 30 September 1918

	Killed in action, died from wounds, died from other causes	Wounded	Missing, including prisoners
France	510,821	1,523,332	236,573
Italy	2,071	4,689	344
Dardanelles	18,688	47,128	7,525
Salonika	9,668	16,837	2,778
Mesopotamia	15,230	19,449	3,581
Egypt	14,763	29,434	2,951
East Africa	1,269	534	62
Afghanistan	120	152	2
North Russia and Vladivostok	359	453	143
Other theatres	508	461	217
Totals	573,497	1,642,469	254,176

Source: *General Annual Reports of the British Army, 1913–1919*,
P.P. 1921, Cmd 1193.

Table 6.6   *Distribution of the British army between*
theatres, 1914–18* ('000s)

	1914	1915	1916	1917	1918
Home	990	1,308	1,542	1,495	1,427
Colonies	56	23	28	27	17
India	68	50	79	83	84
France	213	907	1,379	1,801	1,764
Mediterranean†	–	179	270	–	–
Mesopotamia	–	5	36	73	111
East Africa	–	2	10	10	9
Salonika	–	–	–	208	149
Egypt‡	–	–	–	186	200
Italy	–	–	–	.76	74
Russia	–	–	–	–	4

* On 1 October each year
† Includes Egypt and Gallipoli for 1915 and Egypt and Salonika for 1916
‡ Includes Palestine
Source: *General Annual Reports of the British Army, 1913–1919*,
P.P. 1921, Cmd 1193.

rest, 195 days in quiet sectors, 385 days in active sectors, and only 100 days of actual active operations.[18] It can also be noted that it was not until 1917 that there were more British troops in France and Flanders than in the United Kingdom (Table 6.6). Indeed, through an anomaly in prewar legislation, it was possible to enlist in the Territorial Force for home service only until March 1915. Those who had done so and those prewar Territorials who declined to volunteer for overseas service, amounting to 82,588 men in August 1915, were not compelled to accept overseas service until the passing of the Military Service Acts in January and May 1916. The same legislation also eliminated another provision which enabled prewar Territorials and regulars to seek their discharge at the end of their term of enlistment – evidence suggests that many prewar soldiers exercised that right of discharge until it was finally eradicated.

Judging by the demobilization disturbances, most wartime servicemen simply wished to return to civilian life as soon as possible once the war ended. But, to quote Keith Jeffery, the 'relative buoyancy of recruitment in the post-war period provides little evidence for a general revulsion from warfare or matters military'.[19] The postwar mood towards the army appears one of apathy rather than of antipathy. Could it be then, that for those not actually maimed physically or mentally by the war their wartime service had neither an overtly positive nor an overtly negative impact? Certainly, the anti-war literature, most of which appeared in the period between 1929 and 1935, must be balanced with the published memoirs and accounts of others such as Graham Greenwell or Charles Carrington who did not suffer disillusionment and actually seemed to enjoy the war. Even the literature of disillusionment and the idea of a war generation draws upon the undoubted comradeship generated between men serving together.

If the impact of the war upon the individual was not perhaps as great as has been supposed, it is certainly apparent that the expansion of the army had little impact in the long term. There were changes during the war in the sense that wartime servicemen were civilians first and foremost and brought with them into the army civilian attitudes and values. Working-class men were no less working-class men for being in the army. Indeed, it has been suggested that the mass export of British popular culture to France and the

18 Evelyn Wood, *The Citizen Soldier* (London: privately printed, 1939), p. 49.
19 Keith Jeffery, 'The post-war army', in Beckett and Simpson (eds), *Nation in Arms*, pp. 211-34.

Table 6.7   *Distribution of men between branches of the army on the Western Front, 1914–18**

	1914	1915	1916	1917	1918	1918†
Combatant						
Headquarters	–	–	–	–	1.10	1.15
Cavalry	7.72	3.20	2.55	2.15	0.98	1.01
Royal Horse Artillery & Royal Field Artillery	15.26	11.79	13.09	10.54	11.54	11.40
Royal Garrison Artillery	1.09	2.25	3.58	4.82	6.23	6.47
Royal Engineers	4.92	6.56	9.20	9.54	7.72	7.71
Royal Flying Corps‡	0.49	0.36	0.97	1.49	–	–
Infantry	53.89	57.56	52.17	45.61	33.25	31.90
Cyclist Corps	–	0.64	0.80	0.39	0.34	0.35
Machine Gun Corps	–	–	2.09	2.77	3.72	3.87
Tank Corps	–	–	0.04	0.39	0.84	0.98
Total	83.87	82.36	84.49	77.70	65.72	64.84
Non-Combatant						
Army Service Corps	10.55	11.47	10.19	10.02	9.93	10.38
Royal Army Medical Corps	5.25	4.53	3.37	4.50	3.47	3.44
Army Veterinary Corps	0.26	0.99	1.09	1.03	0.97	0.96
Army Ordnance Corps	0.53	0.60	0.77	0.85	1.16	1.18
Army Pay Corps	0.04	0.05	0.04	0.03	0.04	0.07
Labour Corps	–	–	–	5.83	14.28	14.37
Transportation	–	–	–	–	4.04	4.37
Miscellaneous	–	–	0.05	0.04	0.39	0.39
Total	16.63	17.64	15.51	22.30	34.28	35.16

*   On 1 September each year.
†   On 11 November 1918.
‡   After 1 April 1918 the Royal Flying Corps became the Royal Air Force.

Source: Statistics of the Military Effort of the British Empire (London: HMSO, 1922), pp. 65–6.

distinctly civilian pattern of recreation established behind the lines there helped to maintain British morale while that of other armies cracked. Neither the Territorial Force nor the New Armies adopted quite the same attitude towards military discipline as regulars, the Territorials in particular emphasizing the concept of 'family'. This had its impact after the war when military discipline was modified by the abolition of the degrading Field Punishment No 1 – shackling men to fixed objects such as wheels – in 1923 and the end of the death penalty for all but treachery and mutiny in 1928 and 1929.

The army also embraced the need to recruit more technically skilled personnel in response to the needs of modern war. During the war itself there was a distinct growth in the proportion of what might be termed the non-combatant arms and branches of the service (Table 6.7). The proportion of infantry and cavalry declined while new branches were created such as the Tank Corps, Labour Corps and Machine Gun Corps although only the Tank Corps survived the war. Technical and other educational training was much improved in the army in the postwar years. But all this actually amounted to very little in terms of institutional change after a war of such magnitude. The army contracted rapidly, and by 1922 had fallen below its prewar strength at 217,986 regulars. Moreover, the army's rank and file was recruited from exactly the same sources as the prewar army (Table 6.8). There was a return to that apocryphal state of 'real soldiering', which meant colonial campaigning. No official effort was made to digest the lessons of the war until the establishment of the Kirke Committee in 1932, while in 1926 the Chief of the Imperial General Staff, Sir George Milne , had actually referred to the war as being 'abnormal'. For the military reformer, J. F. C. Fuller, '90 per cent of the army was at work scraping off the reality of war and burnishing up the war-tarnished conventionalities of peace'.[20] In short, the ethos and character of the army had not changed at all as a result of the war.

The key factor was the survival of the old prewar officer class. There had been heavy casualties among prewar regular officers in the earliest campaigns. From a small prewar officer establishment of 12,738, some 3,627 officers had become casualties by November 1914 alone. As a result of such losses and the expansion of the army, an enormous number of commissions were granted, amounting to a total of 229,316. But, of these, only 16,544 were permanent regular commissions: the overwhelming majority were wartime

20 Quoted in Brian Bond, *British Military Policy Between the Two World Wars* (Oxford: Oxford University Press, 1980), p. 36.

temporary commissions, hence the contemporary phrase 'temporary gentlemen'. At first many new officers were drawn from the same elites as prewar officers and, indeed, many were officers 'dug-out' of retirement. A well-known story is that of R. C. Sherriff, author of *Journey's End*, who was denied a commission initially because he had not attended a public school. It made no difference that Sheriff's grammar school had been in existence for some centuries before most of the public schools.[21] Increasingly, however, the social and educational background of candidates for commission declined. Many regulars regarded new officers of the Territorial Force and New Army with a patronizing contempt, although this was one that predated the war in the case of Territorials. It is somewhat ironic that Robert Graves displayed particular hostility to the New Army officers and men in *Goodbye to All That* when he was himself only a wartime officer, albeit one commissioned into the Special Reserve and serving in a regular battalion.

Table 6.8   *Trades of men offering themselves for enlistment, 1906–7, 1912 and 1920 (percentages)*

	1906–7 to 1912–13 five-year average	1920*
Town Casuals	19	19
Agricultural unskilled labour	11	9
Other unskilled labour	17	19
All unskilled labour	47	47
Skilled labour	23	29
Other occupations (semi-skilled)	25	21
Professions, students	1	1
Boys under 17	4	2
Total (%)	100	100
Total number	47,763	68,235

* The only postwar figures available are those for the period 1 January to 30 September 1920.
Source: General Annual Reports of the British Army for the years in question.

Throughout the war, higher command and staff appointments were monopolized by surviving regulars. In March 1917, for example, the War Office took some pride in claiming that the percentage of

21 R. C. Sherriff, 'The English public schools in the war', in G. A. Panichas (ed.), *Promise of Greatness* (London: Cassell, 1968), p. 136.

candidates from the New Army and Territorials taking up places on staff courses at 35.3 per cent collectively exceeded the percentage of candidates from the regular army and the Dominions (31.3 and 33.3 per cent respectively). In fact its significance was that the vastly smaller number of regular officers still commanded such a proportion of places.[22] This does not necessarily imply that all relationships between regular and temporary officers were bad, and many temporary officers were clearly impressed by the regulars to the extent that they emulated them as much as possible. What it does imply is that the perceptions of the officer corps as a whole remained those of the prewar regular and the military direction of the war itself reflected the particular weaknesses of the prewar military mind in adapting to the changes taking place in warfare. Some younger regular officers did learn the lessons of the war and applied them when they, in turn, rose to high command in the Second World War. But, in general, the postwar officer was even more introverted and isolated from society than his prewar predecessor. It was a more technically aware army in 1918 than it had been in 1914 but any more general changes in society which might have occurred as a result of the war simply passed the army by.

This essay began with a list of ways in which the expansion of the British army during the First World War might have been expected to result in lasting institutional change. In reality, there was little change. The army was more truly a 'nation in arms' between 1914 and 1918 than before the war but it was still not representative of society as a whole, even with the introduction of conscription. It is not safe to assume too much of the experience of war for the individual from the perspective of a handful of well-known but not necessarily representative writers. Indeed, the long-term impact of the war upon those who experienced it in the front line may well have been exaggerated. As an institution, the army was not noticeably any different in 1921 from what it had been in 1912 or 1913. From the evidence of the British army, therefore, it might be concluded that, if wars change societies, they change them more than they change the armies that defend those societies.

22 *Hansard*, vol. 90, HC Deb, 5s., 1 March 1917, cols 2197, 2229–31; vol. 91, HC Deb, 5s., 5 March 1917, col. 78.

7

British Politics
and the Great War

JOHN TURNER

INTRODUCTION

The immediately visible consequences of war for the British political system were indeed very great. In 1914 there were four active political parties. Parliament was dominated by the Liberals, who had been in office since 1906, and by the Conservatives, who despite losing three elections in a row still had 272 seats in Parliament, one more than the Liberals. Liberal dominance was secured by alliances with the two minor parties: 42 Labour MPs, mostly from northern industrial constituencies, and 84 Irish Nationalists could be relied upon to support the government against a Conservative opposition. The Liberal Cabinet was capable and determined. An election was expected in 1915, which either major party might have won. By the end of the war this four-party system had been replaced by a three-party system. The Liberal Party, temporarily broken in two, had been reduced to a second-class party. Labour had grown in numbers and extended its geographical range. The Conservative Party, swollen by the general election of 1918, had become the party of the capitalist class. The Irish Nationalist Party had disappeared from the face of politics. These changes were never reversed, and it is difficult not to conclude that the Great War had, to use a more modern phrase, 'broken the mould' of the nineteenth-century party system. Moreover, the war's impact on politics went far beyond its effects on the parties. Popular attitudes to the class structure and the role of the state were shaken. The British electoral system was transformed into a fair approximation of democracy, with all adult males and most women enfranchised. At every level, the discontinuities in political history are at the forefront. To understand these changes we must first look at the development of parliamentary politics during the war, then at the influence of the war on the electorate.

THE END OF LIBERAL HEGEMONY

The first casualty of the rising flood was the Liberal government itself. After a landslide victory in 1906, the Liberal administration had passed more reforming legislation than any government before it. Since 1908 it had been led by H. H. Asquith, once associated with the Liberal Imperialists on the right wing of the party, with vigorous support from David Lloyd George, the Chancellor of the Exchequer, a more flamboyant and radical figure. The other leading light of the ministry was Winston Churchill, who had started his political life as a Conservative, switched to the Liberals in 1904, and reached Cabinet office in 1908. Until 1910 the Liberals' huge majority had protected them from serious challenge, but the two elections of that year reduced them to dependence on their parliamentary allies, and their talent for producing vigorous, popular and effective legislation seemed to run out. After the 1911 National Insurance Act, which was divisive even within the party, the Liberals lost their luck. The third Home Rule Bill, introduced in 1912, nearly caused a civil war in Ireland because Unionists in Ulster were determined to resist it. Industrial relations were particularly bad between 1911 and 1913, and the government was drawn in as never before. The naval arms race with Germany cost money which many Liberals would have preferred to spend on social programmes. In July 1914 the Cabinet was riven by its recent disagreements about the budget, and afraid of the breakdown of civil order in Ireland. In the country, Liberal activists who would have to bear the burden of the general election campaign of 1915 were grumbling about the 'socialistic' tendencies of recent legislation.

Small wonder, then, that Asquith, reflecting early in 1915 on the August crisis, congratulated himself on the '*Luck* [which] helped you in external things .... above all (at a most critical and fateful moment in your career) in the sudden outbreak of the Great War'. At the time he simply told the Chief Whip that 'God moves in mysterious ways, his wonders to perform'. The war enabled the Cabinet to forget about Ireland and the disestablishment of the Welsh Church, to bring about a 'political truce' which protected them against Conservative attack, and to smother the opposition of their own supporters. Patriotism and national unity would enable the government to avoid its political troubles until Christmas, by which time the war might be over.[1] But the war was not over by Christmas, and this drastic cure for Liberal ailments turned out to be worse than the disease. It was surprisingly easy to overcome the scruples of Cabinet opponents of the decision to go to war. Most ministers wanted to go to war because they believed that it was in Britain's interest to resist Germany's bid for European domination. Most of the rest were persuaded by the specious argument that Germany had violated Belgian neutrality. John Morley and John Burns resigned in protest. But then the problems began. The government's plans for war assumed that Britain would send a small expeditionary force to France and exert most of its power in a naval blockade of Germany. Otherwise it was to be 'business as usual', with industry and commerce at home carrying on as before to provide the economic strength which this strategy required.[2] Instead there was military stalemate, with political consequences which were apparent by the end of 1914.

Asquith had brought in Lord Kitchener, a soldier rather than a politician, to be Secretary of State for War, largely to inspire public confidence. Kitchener expected a European war to last three or more years and to require a huge land army, whose members would have to be drawn from the ranks of industrial workers. By Christmas 1914 some ministers, including Winston Churchill at the Admiralty, wanted to find another theatre of war in the Near or Middle East to get round the apparently invincible German lines in the west.[3] While the Cabinet doubted its own direction, public and parliamentary confidence in the government was beginning to waver, and the Conservative Party in particular was chafing at the limitations of the 'political truce'. They could not openly criticize the government, lest they were accused of lack of patriotism, but they profoundly distrusted its ability to win the war.

In the spring of 1915 these undercurrents began to pull Asquith's Cabinet down. In February, Lloyd George, the Chancellor of the Exchequer, called into question both the Western Front strategy and the policy of 'business as usual'.[4] The first result of this was a set of agreements with some trade unions and some engineering employers

1 For the Liberals' predicament at the outbreak of war, see Cameron Hazlehurst, *Politicians at War, 1914–1915* (London: Cape, 1971); Patricia Jalland, *The Liberals and Ireland* (Hassocks: Harvester, 1980).
2 See David French, 'The rise and fall of business as usual' in Kathleen Burk, (ed.), *War and the State* (London: Allen & Unwin, 1982).
3 Stephen Roskill, *Hankey, Man of Secrets* (London: Collins, 1970), pp. 146–54, sketches the possibilities advanced.
4 Memorandum by the Chancellor of the Exchequer, 22 February 1915,

to speed up the production of ammunition; these were later known as the 'Treasury Agreements', and reflected Lloyd George's concern that the War Office under Kitchener could not manage the procurement of enough munitions for the new sort of war in the trenches.[5] But the political impact of the Treasury Agreements was trivial compared with the upheaval caused by the failure of the British Army's first major offensive of 1915. Like most subsequent efforts to break the German line by frontal assault, the attack failed, and GHQ in France blamed the shortage of gun ammunition.[6] Staff officers were sent back to England to tell opposition MPs that the government was letting the soldiers down, and a press campaign was launched in the newspapers owned by Lord Northcliffe. This coincided with the resignation on 15 May of Fisher, the First Sea Lord, who opposed the government's policy of attacking Turkey in the Dardanelles. The combination of failure in France and controversy in the Admiralty was too much for the House of Commons. Conservative MPs threatened to defy their leaders and vote against the government. Liberals, many of whom had hesitated even about the decision to go to war, were equally discontented but did not know what to do about it. The prospect of losing a vote of confidence and being forced into a general election was too much even for Asquith's legendary nerve. On the other side the Conservative leader, Bonar Law, did not want to be blamed for causing a political crisis at a moment of national emergency.[7]

The immediate result was the reconstruction of the government. With the help of Lloyd George and Churchill, Asquith brought Bonar Law and a few of his colleagues into a coalition. The new government included Arthur Balfour, the most experienced Conservative statesman, who took over the Admiralty from Churchill; Edward Carson, the Ulster Unionist leader and an outspoken critic of the Asquith government's war policy; Bonar Law himself, who took the rather junior position of Colonial Secretary; and a number of other Conservative leaders. The main Liberal casualties

Public Record Office, Cabinet Papers, CAB 42/1/39.

5 Chris Wrigley, *David Lloyd George and the British Labour Movement* (Hassocks: Harvester, 1976), pp. 102-9.

6 David French, 'The military background to the "shell crisis" of May 1915', *Journal of Strategic Studies*, vol. 2, no. 2 (1979).

7 Hazlehurst, *Politicians at War*, pp. 227–305; M.D. Pugh, 'Asquith, Bonar Law and the First Coalition', *Historical Journal*, vol. 17, no. 4 (1974). On the 'drink scandal', which lent a comic air to the proceedings, see John Turner, 'State purchase of the liquor trade in the First World War', *Historical Journal*, vol. 23, no. 3 (1980).

were Lord Haldane, accused of pro-Germanism by the Conservative backwoodsmen, and Churchill, who was blamed for failures
in the Dardanelles. Lloyd George moved from the Treasury to the
newly created Ministry of Munitions, and Asquith remained firmly
in 10 Downing Street.

THE ASQUITH COALITION

The hasty exit of the Liberal Cabinet was not at first seen as a rout
for the Liberal Party. Asquith had stacked the odds against Conservative influence in the new administration: most of the important
offices were still held by Liberals, including the Treasury and the
Foreign Office. There were plenty of accusations of conspiracy and
double-dealing, but the worst that could at first be said of the new
government was that it was a conspiracy of the front benches against
the back. Asquith and Bonar Law had seen a common interest in
preventing a crisis and a general election. The trouble began when
backbenchers on both sides realized what had happened. The anti-
war minority among Liberal MPs now decided that they could attack
a 'mongrel coalition' with a clear conscience.[8] On the other side
the more belligerent Conservatives soon realized that they had been
tricked. Asquith and most of his Liberal colleagues were determined
to resist their opponents' most cherished policies.

The Conservatives as they entered the coalition were determined
to wind up the Dardanelles expedition and to force the government
to accept military conscription. These were the major political issues of late 1915 but, until October, Asquith managed to contain
them both. Conservative opposition to the Dardanelles expedition
was overcome in August, and the groundswell of conscription clam-
our was ignored. But within the new Cabinet Lloyd George took
the lead in calling for military conscription as a matter of urgency,
allying himself with the Conservatives. In October a compromise –
the Derby scheme – was brought into operation. It failed, and the
conscriptionists pressed for undisguised compulsion. Amid threats
of Liberal resignation and counter-threats by Conservatives to wreck
the ministry, Asquith tried to keep his balance. In December he finally gave in and a limited Military Service Act was passed, calling
up only single men. Sir John Simon, alone, resigned. Even this
measure did not satisfy Lloyd George and the Conservatives, and
further pressure was brought until by May 1916 the Liberals in the

8 See Michael Bentley, *The Liberal Mind* (Cambridge: Cambridge University Press, 1977), pp. 24–37.

Cabinet were forced to accept the conscription of married men and an extension of the age limits.

The Dardanelles also took its toll on the ministry's shaky unity. With the outspoken support of the generals, most Conservatives continued to demand British withdrawal and the concentration of men and resources on the Western Front. The decision to pull out was taken in December, after months of military and naval humiliation, and carried out in the first days of the new year. Because of these disagreements over war policy, the temper of the coalition was never good. Suspicion, press leaks, and overt lobbying spread ill-feeling throughout Westminster. Lloyd George was particularly vulnerable to charges from Liberal backbenchers, encouraged by his Liberal opponents in Cabinet, that he was plotting to overthrow either Asquith or Liberal principles or both. Everything he did to urge conscription made suspicion worse, and even pro-war Liberals feared for Liberal unity. The government was not helped by the lack of any spectacular victories to count against the humiliation in the Dardanelles.[9]

The Dublin rising on Easter Monday 1916, undertaken by a few members of the Irish Republican Brotherhood, could therefore hardly have come at a worse time. The rebellion itself was quickly suppressed. Rather than letting matters lie, and opening up negotiations with moderate Irish Nationalists to make sure it never happened again, the government allowed the military authorities to carry out a ferocious campaign of summary executions. The Cabinet also authorized the trial and execution of Sir Roger Casement, who had been caught red-handed in an attempt to link the rising to Germany. Only then, with Irish opinion thoroughly inflamed, did the government set up discussions with the Irish Nationalists and the Ulster Unionists which were intended to bring about a permanent settlement of the Irish question. These talks, led by Lloyd George, moved quickly. Carson for the Unionists and John Redmond for the Nationalists agreed that Ireland would be partitioned, giving Home Rule to the South and leaving the North in the United Kingdom. Unfortunately, the deal was not first cleared with the Conservatives in the Cabinet. When it was brought to the full Cabinet for ratification Walter Long and Lord Lansdowne fell upon it and rallied their Conservative colleagues to veto it. This left no one happy. Conservative backbenchers were furious with Asquith and even more furious with those of their leaders who had not resisted him from the first.

9 There is no satisfactory study of this period in First World War politics: John Grigg's *Lloyd George: From Peace to War* (London: Methuen, 1985) is the best recent biographical approach to it.

Liberals saw partition as a 'sell out' to Ulster. The Irish Nationalist Party was humiliated, and Irish public opinion soon turned to the more radical separatist Sinn Fein movement, with profound consequences for the future.[10]

By the autumn of 1916 the Asquith Coalition was beginning to look terminally ill. Conscription and Ireland had taken their toll of parliamentary confidence. Withdrawal from the Dardanelles shook public opinion, and during 1916 the abortive naval battle of Jutland and the defeat and surrender of the British expeditionary force in Mesopotamia further eroded national confidence. The year 1916 also produced the first signs that Britain's civilian population might not be able to last the war out. Widespread strikes in engineering centres in the Spring were caused by inflation, especially of food prices, and discontent about conscription and the 'dilution' of skilled labour with female and semi-skilled male workers. The harvest was bad, and by the end of the year most of the country's financial and supply problems were getting very much worse. On the Western Front the battle of the Somme was a spectacular and bloody failure, though the public was not allowed to know its magnitude. Within the government, in November, Lord Lansdowne suggested an early peace, before too much damage was done.

This was a moment of crisis. Asquith was personally opposed to an early peace, but many of his colleagues who shared this view did not believe that he could win the war. Carson, now out of the ministry, was prepared to attack the government in Parliament, and on 8 November he was able to persuade a significant number of Conservative backbenchers to oppose the government in the Nigeria debate. This was an open warning to Conservatives still in the government that their time was nearly up. Lloyd George, responding to Lansdowne's pessimism, made an unauthorized public declaration of the importance of fighting on until Germany could be given a 'knockout blow', and opened discussions with Carson and Bonar Law to force a reconstruction of the ministry. By the end of November the inner cabinet was polarized. Asquith and some of his Liberal supporters were on one side; Lloyd George, Bonar Law and (by implication) almost all the other Conservatives were on the other. Asquith tried to deal with this by calling his opponents' bluff and resigning, but found, rather to his astonishment, that Lloyd George could not only form a ministry but hold it together.

10 Michael Laffan, 'The unification of Sinn Fein in 1917', *Irish Historical Studies*, vol. 17, no. 67 (1971) gives some attention to this. See also D. Fitzpatrick, *Politics and Irish Life* (Dublin: Gill Macmillan, 1977).

On 6 December the new regime took over and survived until the end of the war.[11]

THE LLOYD GEORGE COALITION

The Lloyd George Coalition was an odd phenomenon. Its parliamentary support was mostly Conservative. Throughout the war Bonar Law was loyal to Lloyd George, and managed to impose his will on colleagues who had a longer political experience than his. Most of the Liberal ministers went with Asquith, leaving most of the jobs to Conservatives. Also included in the ministry were a small but representative number of Labour leaders under Arthur Henderson, who had been the token Labour member of the Asquith Coalition. The new coalition should have enjoyed much wider and less complicated support than its predecessor, but clearly it did not. Where the Asquith Coalition tripped up over conscription and state intervention in the economy, the Lloyd George Coalition had even more fundamental problems in managing the war economy and preventing economic disaster. When it took office the dollar exchange was about to collapse and Britain was faced with a technical bankruptcy over its purchases of munitions, food and raw materials from the United States.[12] The problem of the Western Front was now acute. The ostensible purpose of Lloyd George's bid to reorganize the machinery of government was to reimpose civilian control over strategy. He was afraid that if wasteful offensives were repeated it would prove impossible to survive, and that Lansdowne's predictions would come true. Social unrest and the withdrawal of consent by the industrial working classes were real dangers. In fact Lloyd George had been hoist by his own petard. The present discontents had been caused by policies which he had pressed on his colleagues in 1916, and were reinforced by the dominant position of the generals in military planning, which he had until recently supported. Now the generals wanted to repeat the offensive which had failed in 1916, and whichever way the government turned to mitigate the consequences it met some sort of opposition.[13]

11 The extensive literature on this episode is discussed in John Turner's forthcoming *British Politics and the Crisis of War* (London: Yale University Press).
12 Kathleen Burk, *Britain, America and the Sinews of War* (London: Allen & Unwin, 1985), pp. 76–95.
13 David Woodward, *Lloyd George and the Generals* (London: Associated University Presses, 1983), is the most complete recent account.

Lloyd George's first concern was to improve the domestic organization of war. He set up a small War Cabinet. Its members – himself, Henderson, Bonar Law and two Conservative peers, Curzon and Milner – sat almost daily to oversee the administration, and departmental ministers had no seat in Cabinet. New departments for shipping, food, food production, national service, and labour were created in an enormous hurry. Some of these were successful, some not, though their success could not really be measured until after the end of the war. In war policy Lloyd George tried to force the generals to accept new tactical methods, though this merely resulted in the fiasco of the Nivelle offensive in the spring of 1917 and, in turn, in a mutiny in the French army which left Britain fighting virtually alone on the Western Front. After this it was impossible to prevent Haig from trying his favoured frontal offensive through Flanders which led to the even more disastrous Passchendaele campaign.

At home the political situation was never stable. After a 'honeymoon period' for a few weeks after the opening of the new parliamentary session the government was faced by its first challenge from Liberal MPs who objected to the imposition of tariffs on cotton goods entering India. After this, Liberal opposition to Lloyd George grew steadily and, although he always had the support of the majority of Liberals in Parliament, the anti-war Liberals who had criticized Asquith gradually came to support the displaced Asquithians in a common front against Lloyd George.[14]

Only because Asquith declined at first to attack the new government did some sort of political truce survive in Parliament in the early part of 1917. As the year wore on a solid core of opposition could be discerned, consisting of half a dozen Labour MPs and about a hundred Liberals. It could never be enough to challenge the government's majority, unless a significant section of the Conservative Party deserted the government. This had brought Asquith down; Lloyd George and his colleagues feared that the same might happen to them.

The immediate threat to the government, though, was more fundamental. In the conduct of the war 1917 was like 1916, but more so. Military success was elusive. At home, raw materials and basic foodstuffs were in short supply. In industry, more and more skilled men were being taken for the army and replaced by women and unskilled male workers. This was resented, especially when em-

14 Edward David, 'The Liberal Party divided, 1916-1918', *Historical Journal*, vol. 13, no. 3 (1970); M. Hart, 'The Liberal decline in Parliament and the constituencies' unpublished DPhil thesis, Oxford University, 1982.

ployers seemed to be making huge profits while workers gave up the prewar working practices which had protected their wages and independence. The Spring strikes of 1916 were repeated in 1917. Engineering workers in Coventry, Sheffield and Liverpool downed tools in protest against the conscription of skilled men, new working practices, and the emerging problem that skilled engineers sometimes earned less than the semi-skilled production workers on piece rates. But an ominous foreign example now changed the language of the strikers and the perceptions of the government.

In March the Tsarist regime in Russia had been toppled by the first Russian Revolution. The Provisional Government in Russia was a mild, fairly progressive group of liberal individuals, who promised to go on fighting the war against Germany; but behind them was a movement of protest whose full strength could only be guessed. News reached Britain of Workers' and Soldiers' Councils to protest against the war and call for an immediate 'democratic' peace. These soon found imitators. Respectable British trade unionists began to call themselves Bolshevists; the War Cabinet began to make plans in case Russia withdrew from the war. Their other fear was that the strike movement would follow the Russian example, uniting discontented workers with discontented soldiers in an attempt to stop the war. Swift moves were made to end the strikes by arresting and deporting the ringleaders. Fairly generous terms were offered as a face-saver to the official trade union leaders who had been forced to support the rank and file demands for strike action. The government quickly set up a Commission on Industrial Unrest, which soon concluded that high food prices and the suspicion of profiteering had contributed most to the support for the strikes. But no one could be certain that anti-war feeling would not take hold. In May 1917 a group of trades councils and peace groups, including some indigenous 'Workers and Soldiers Councils' which had sprung up, called a meeting in Leeds which was dubbed the 'Leeds Soviet'.[15] Speeches were made calling for an immediate cessation of fighting and a 'democratic peace' with 'no annexations or indemnities' – an echo of the demands being made in Russia. Although the Leeds Soviet did not agree on a concerted plan, and revealed considerable divisions even in that self-selected group, it was a portent of the future.

These stirrings led to a new interest in the attitudes of labour and the Labour Party. At the outbreak of war the Labour Party had

15 Stephen White, 'Soviets in Britain: the Leeds Convention of 1917', *International Review of Social History*, vol. 19, no. 3 (1974).

split. The chairman of the parliamentary party, Ramsay MacDonald, moved to oppose the war but was defeated by the majority of his colleagues and resigned to lead an anti-war minority socialist group, dominated by members of the Independent Labour Party. The majority of Labour MPs, especially those sponsored by trade unions, supported the war and elected Arthur Henderson as their leader. This pattern of a pro-war majority and an anti-war minority was common to socialist and labour parties all over Europe. The Asquith Coalition made half-hearted attempts to incorporate the majority Labour Party into government by appointing Henderson to the nominal post of President of the Board of Education. Lloyd George, when making up his government in December 1916, had gone much further, making promises about postwar reconstruction, putting Henderson in the War Cabinet, and giving ministerial posts to a number of Labour MPs. But despite its divisions the Labour Party had stayed together. Majority and minority leaders co-operated on the National Executive Committee of the party. Through the local trades councils and the War Emergency Workers National Committee the party had done a great deal to represent working-class interests over welfare questions and matters such as housing, soldiers pensions, separation allowances for soldiers' families, and so on.[16] Most important of all, the party had retained its interest in international questions and preserved an independent identity as part of an international socialist movement. In the new circumstances of 1917, this became a matter of high significance.

One of the British government's first moves towards the new Russian government was to send Arthur Henderson to Russia in the hope that, as a Labour man, he could speak directly to the radical and socialist elements in the new government, and find out what they wanted and were likely to do. Henderson was sent to Russia to keep Russia in the war. Once there, he saw the depth of the discontent, and was afraid. While he was in Russia, in June 1917, a suggestion emerged from the Russian socialists that an international conference of socialist parties from all belligerent countries should meet in Stockholm to discuss ways of putting pressure on their respective governments to bring the war to a close. Henderson decided that this was a good thing, and that unless something like it was done there was a serious risk that Britain would go the same way as Russia. He returned to England, and began to work with Ramsay

16 R. Harrison, 'The War Emergency Workers National Committee', in A. Briggs and J. Saville (eds), *Essays in Labour History*, vol 2, (London: Macmillan, 1971).

MacDonald to prepare for the conference, making arrangements first with socialist parties from the Allied countries. Lloyd George, at first, was keen to see the meeting go ahead, but Conservatives in the War Cabinet wanted to veto it and their views prevailed. On 11 August, Henderson chose to ignore their advice and recommended to a national conference of the Labour Party that delegates should be sent to Stockholm. He was immediately forced to resign from the War Cabinet and replaced by the more compliant George Barnes.[17]

This was a turning-point for Labour. Although the government had an easy parliamentary victory over the Stockholm affair, and although the pro-war elements in the Labour movement did prevent Labour delegates from taking part in any conferences which might involve them in meeting German socialists, the challenge of a 'democratic' peace was there. From August onwards the government was under growing pressure to justify the sacrifices which were being made for the war. At the same time, the leaders of the Labour Party were preparing themselves as a fully fledged opposition.

As Labour's leaders thought, a general election during the war was always a possibility. The House of Commons was very long in the tooth, with no popular mandate since 1910. Lloyd George and his colleagues were convinced that public opinion was solidly behind the government, much more so than the Commons. The temptation to clear opposition out of the way in a khaki election was very strong, even though it would involve delicate negotiations between the Conservative and Liberal wings of the Coalition. Election matters were first discussed in Lloyd George's immediate circle in May 1917. In the autumn the pressure grew stronger, for a number of reasons. The government was afraid that there would be food shortages over the winter. The war in France was going nowhere, and Lloyd George wanted to be in a strong political position to confront the generals and force them to change their tactics. Asquith was beginning to exert himself, for the first time, as an opposition leader, and using as an issue the cry of 'Hands off the generals', which had dangerous resonances on the Conservative side of the House. Lloyd George and Christopher Addison, his principal Liberal colleague, decided in October that the time had come for a positive move to improve the government's image in preparation for an election.

In November a new factor tipped the balance further towards an election. Lord Lansdowne, who had been out of government since

17 J.M. Winter, 'Arthur Henderson, the Russian Revolution, and the leadership of the Labour Party', *Historical Journal*, vol. 15, no. 4, (1972).

December 1916, wrote to the press to urge that some effort be made to come to terms with Germany before the war destroyed British society. His defeatism was utterly conservative: he did not like what he saw of the social changes of wartime, the new power of the trade unions, the threat of high taxation, and the implicit attack on the landed classes. He was merely making public what he had said in private to his Cabinet colleagues a year before, but he struck a raw nerve. The government was already afraid of being forced to make a premature peace by the defection of Russia, which had just suffered its second, Bolshevik revolution. Lansdowne's letter was welcomed in many officers' messes in France because of the very conservative implications of what he said and because many serving soldiers could see no prospect of clear military victory. At the other end of the political spectrum, members of the Independent Labour Party and radical anti-war Liberals saw this as an expression of sanity from an unlikely quarter. Asquith's Liberal colleagues encouraged him to support it, though he was personally very reluctant to do so. The government was forced to make plans to outflank any broad coalition of political forces intent on an early peace.

The first move was to present British war aims in a light which was more acceptable to 'democratic' instincts, while giving nothing away. This was achieved by Lloyd George in his Caxton Hall speech on 6 January, which was addressed to an audience of trade unionists. The clear message was that Britain's aims were moderate and just. They also conformed to the war aims of the United States, which were soon to be set out by President Wilson in his famous Fourteen Points. The Caxton Hall speech was a success, if success can be judged by the response of the deeply reactionary *Morning Post*, which called it defeatist.[18] Meanwhile the Liberal and Conservative political organizers on the government side were beginning to draw up a list of parliamentary constituencies to be shared out in a wartime election, and the heads of a joint election programme which would rally all patriotic voters behind the war coalition, with an additional promise of social reform in the early months of peace to deflect voters from the Labour Party. The major obstacle to an early election was the Representation of the People Bill, a far-reaching measure of franchise reform which had been agreed by all parties in 1916 and which would increase the size of the electorate by about 2.5 times. It was seen as unreasonable to hold an election on the old franchise when the new franchise, based on agreed principles, was so near to

18 David R. Woodward, 'The origins and intent of David Lloyd George's January 5 War Aims speech', *The Historian*, vol. 24, no. 4 (1971).

completion. Plans were therefore made to hold an election as soon as a new register was complete, probably in the summer of 1918.[19]

THE CRISIS OF MARCH–MAY 1918

These plans were diverted by the Germans. The German spring offensive which began on 21 March threw the British army back for miles. Simply to avoid defeat the government was forced to divert all available men to the Western Front, and passed a new Military Service Act which extended the age limits upwards to 51 and reduced the number of 'reserved occupations'. The most damaging feature of this legislation was that for the first time conscription was extended to Ireland, which had been exempt in the past for the very good reason that Irish loyalty was in doubt. Opposition was intense, and came at a very awkward moment, since for nearly a year an 'Irish Convention' had been sitting which was on the point of producing a compromise agreement which might have settled the Irish Question for good. Instead, the Convention broke up in disarray, and the majority of the Nationalist Party, which had preserved a tattered dignity because of its presence on the Convention, rushed headlong into the arms of Sinn Fein. To prevent a total breakdown of law and order in Ireland, the government offered to link Irish conscription with the promise of Home Rule. Now there was an explosion in the House of Commons, as Conservatives realized that their Unionist principles were being sold down the river. What had begun as an emergency measure to raise troops precipitated a major crisis for the Coalition, which faced defeat at the hands of an unholy alliance of Irish Nationalists, anti-conscriptionists, Conservative Unionists and discontented Asquithian Liberals.[20]

Into this already complicated scene stepped the soldierly figure of Sir Frederick Maurice. Maurice had until recently been the Director of Military Operations, a senior staff post at the War Office which gave him responsibility for troop movements and the allocation of men in the army. In May 1918 he had two firm beliefs. The first was that the War Cabinet was systematically and covertly starving the army of men for the Western Front. This was true: the decision had been taken in August 1917, because ministers believed that the economy could stand no more drains of men but, on the

19 See the general discussion in M.D. Pugh, *Electoral Reform in War and Peace* (London: Routledge and Kegan Paul, 1978).
20 A.J. Ward, 'David Lloyd George and the Irish conscription crisis', *Historical Journal*, vol. 17, no.1 (1974).

other hand, that the government could not stand the political row if it acknowledged that it was holding troops back from the front. General Maurice's second belief was that the Prime Minister was a liar. This was also true, but it did not follow from these two premisses, as General Maurice believed, that Lloyd George had lied to the House of Commons about troop strengths in France. This, however, was what Maurice decided he had to make public, and he did so by writing to the newspapers. This had worked for Lansdowne, and there was no reason why it should not work for him.[21]

The result, as he expected, was a parliamentary storm. For the first time Asquith came out in open opposition to the government. The Conservative back benches, which shared General Maurice's opinion of Lloyd George and were also by instinct defenders of generals, were out for blood. This was the most severe test of the Lloyd George Coalition's strength. On the day, 9 May, the Coalition won: only 106 Liberal and Labour members and one renegade Conservative voted against the government. Lloyd George managed to persuade the House that he had not been lying, and Asquith bungled his attack.

The Maurice Debate is generally reckoned as a historic moment in British politics. An American observer saw in it the appearance of a 'new opposition' of radical liberals and anti-war socialists. The Coalition's organizers used the date of the Maurice Debate as a test in deciding whether or not individual Liberal MPs were supporters of the government: MPs who had voted against the government on or before 9 May were opposed in the December election, even if they had subsequently changed their ways. But at the time its significance was very different. On the evening before the debate the Unionist War Committee, an organization of Tory backbench MPs and peers, discussed the issues. Most wanted at first to vote against the government because of its Irish policy. The argument that tipped the meeting in favour of supporting the government, and thus preserved the Coalition in office, was that even if Ireland had to be sacrificed it was essential to keep Asquith out of the premiership.[22]

All this was duly reported to Lloyd George. One view frequently expressed in his inner circle was that the Maurice Debate was part of a military plot against the government, involving senior officers who were sympathetic to the Irish Unionist cause. This rumour, though it might seem far-fetched, is corroborated. Lord Gorell, a

21 Nancy Spears, (ed.), *The Maurice Case* (London: Leo Cooper, 1972).
22 *The Leo Amery Diaries*, John Barnes and David Nicholson (eds), vol. 1 (London: Hutchinson, 1980), pp. 219-20.

young staff officer, recorded in his diary that in February he had been sent over from France to discover whether there were any serious candidates to replace Lloyd George as prime minister. Directly after the debate, General Sir Henry Rawlinson, the British military representative at the Supreme War Council in Versailles, mentioned the existence of such a plot in his diary, linking it with Carson and a number of the more notoriously right-wing generals. Quite apart from the army's losses, and its fear for Lloyd George's impact on postwar society, the army hierarchy was offended by Lloyd George's recent brusque dismissal of Sir William Robertson from the position of Chief of the Imperial General Staff. Robertson had resisted the government's proposals to put the British army's reserves in France under Allied control, and had been levered out of office in the middle of February. The Unionist War Committee had on that occasion echoed the soldiers' resentment of Lloyd George's intervention.

Another implicit message for Lloyd George was that he could rely on Conservative support only as long as the war lasted. It was now in his interest to hasten an election which his supporters would fight as a coalition. Preparations for an election therefore dominated the political scene from May onwards. For the first time since 1914, British politics seemed to go on without looking over its shoulder to what was going on in France. Had the politicians bothered to look, they would have seen a momentous conclusion to the war, as two armoured dinosaurs competed to reach extinction first. In the event the German dinosaur was the first to collapse; but by then the politicians had their eyes firmly on the electoral future.

THE COUPON ELECTION

Liberal and Conservative organizers now divided up the seats, with some argument. Conservative supporters of the Coalition were automatically to be returned: Liberals whose record was satisfactory were also safe. The half-dozen Labour MPs who had opposed the war were to be challenged, the 'patriotic' section of the party being left alone. A programme was knocked together, consisting of a minimum of social reform proposals which the two sides could mutually accept. This would all have gone ahead whether or not the war was finished, but in the event, on 6 November, five days before the Armistice, Lloyd George went to the king asking for a dissolution on the grounds that it was essential to have a quick election before postwar discontent took hold. His request was granted, the campaign was opened on 14 November, and the country went to the polls on 14 December. Every Coalition candidate received a letter of support signed jointly by Lloyd George and Bonar Law, rudely nicknamed the 'Coupon' by opposition Liberals.

The result was a triumph for the Coalition. The Asquithian Liberals were reduced to thirty-eight seats. The Labour Party, which had decided at the last minute not to be associated with the Coalition, took sixty seats, many of which were won with the tacit consent of the Coalition. The Coalition itself took 537 seats, of which 127 went to Liberals. This outcome is more difficult to assess than appears at first sight. Labour's modest improvement in representation in the Commons reflected a large increase in the number of its candidates: in terms of votes cast per candidate, and allowing for the large increase in the electorate, the party hardly did better than in 1910. The Conservatives clearly did well, and would almost certainly have done so without the Coupon, for some of their candidates defeated couponed Liberals. For the Liberal Party the allocation of coupons seemed to crystallize the divisions in the party which had first appeared in 1916 and had become impossible to ignore by the time of the Maurice Debate. Although most of the uncouponed 'Asquithian' candidates protested their support for the Coalition's programme, and a high proportion of those elected were friendly or at least neutral towards the Coalition in the new Parliament, the split in the party which had been imposed by the organizers at Westminster demoralized local Liberal parties and enraged the victims of the Coupon. Controversies in the postwar Parliament further divided the party; and when the Coalition finally fell, in 1922, Liberals were still squabbling. Although the Liberal–Conservative alliance had by then collapsed, the two wings of the Liberal Party still fought the election separately, and the party's share of the total vote shrank further during the 1920s. In 1922 the Labour Party put up fewer candidates than the Liberals, but got more votes and more seats: 142 against 115 for the two Liberal wings combined. By then it was clear that 1918 had been the beginning of the end for the Liberals and at least the end of the beginning for Labour.

The year 1918 was also the end for the Irish Nationalist Party, which was reduced to seven seats, one of them in England and five, ironically, in Ulster. Its place had been taken by the separatist Sinn Fein movement, whose candidates had begun to win seats in by-elections after the collapse of the Lloyd George initiative in 1916. The conscription crisis in March and April 1918 had sealed the fate of the Nationalists, who had proved impotent to resist English tyranny over Ireland. Sinn Fein MPs refused to attend the Westminster Parliament, and without an Irish element in British politics the Irish Question, as it had been understood before the war, ceased to exist. It was replaced by an increasingly bloody revolution in the South of Ireland, which was only brought to an end by British withdrawal in 1921.

THE TWILIGHT OF LIBERALISM

And so, with a landslide election, the politics of war came to an end. At first sight it seems obvious that the Liberal Party, for one, had been struck a mortal blow by the 'rampant omnibus' of war. But it is not enough to say that the war was 'incompatible with Liberal principles' and leave it at that. It had certainly not been a simple split between the pure-in-heart Liberals and the compromisers who embraced the war. The party had been divided before 1914. Social policy, foreign policy and Ireland had been important issues, and the brew was seasoned with personal antagonisms. In these respects the Liberals were hardly worse off than their Tory opponents, who had sacked their leader in 1911 and nearly cut themselves in two over Tariff Reform in the ten years before 1913. When the Liberal cabinet entered the war it was criticized by the same backbench Liberal MPs who had protested in 1911 that the foreign policy of Sir Edward Grey was no better than Conservative foreign policy.

The minority Liberals were strengthened during the next few months by MPs who objected as a matter of principle to the extension of state control in the economy, and this enlarged group of disaffected MPs constituted the main opposition to the Asquith coalition. But at no time did the Liberal Cabinet members stand on this sort of principle in their resistance to conscription or economic controls. Their objection was based instead on the fear that conscription would swell the size of the army beyond the number which could be supported by the men left behind in industry: considerations of individual liberty were not important. As a result the radical minority on the Liberal back benches, itself united only by its dislike of the government's policy, was highly critical of Liberal Cabinet members. Although Lloyd George was the most hated Liberal minister, his Cabinet opponents, such as Reginald McKenna and Walter Runciman, were also distrusted by the minority. So was Asquith. When Asquith left the government, accompanied by McKenna, Runciman and almost every other Liberal minister, he was greeted coolly by his erstwhile opponents in the party, and for the rest of the war there were three main Liberal factions, not two. When both of the anti-Lloyd George factions could be persuaded to vote on the same side, as they did in the Maurice Debate and in some lesser divisions in the autumn of 1917, they could muster about a hundred members between them. This was substantially less than half the number of Liberal MPs usually present at Westminster. The majority of Liberal MPs supported the government – all governments – throughout the war.

Nor did the lines of division represent a simple ideological split between left and right in the party. A number of the prominent 'New Liberals' of the Edwardian years were opposed to the war and in time opposed to Lloyd George because of his belligerent attitudes. But their social values were not shared by the Cobdenite 'Liberal millionaires' who formed the core of the resistance to state intervention in 1915, nor by Asquith. On the other side of the divide, Christopher Addison and Alfred Mond represented an advanced and constructive Liberalism which influenced the Coalition's postwar reconstruction programme. Perhaps no attempt should be made to reduce the divisions in the Liberal Party, even at parliamentary level, to an orderly pattern. The only simplification which does not do violence to the facts is to say that personal disagreements among the leaders over war policy made sure that ordinary disputes in the party were aggravated when they might otherwise have been healed.

This failure of leadership destroyed the party's ability to fight an election in 1918. The routine organization of the party was disrupted by the war, as agents and activists left for war work. After December 1916, Asquith's whips and Lloyd George's whips competed for the loyalties of local parties, but by December 1918 many local organizations were moribund. *Ad hoc* committees, got up to choose a candidate, were confused by the apparently arbitrary use of the Coupon. Canvassing was poor or nonexistent. Asquith's supporters found it hard to follow or even understand him when he insisted that he and his friends supported the Coalition's programme but not the Coalition. Uncouponed Liberals, including Asquith himself and most of his closest associates, suffered heavy defeats. The sense of failure was lasting. In 1922, after some turbulent years for the party under the Coalition government, the two factions still could not agree to co-operate and the electorate was evidently beginning to despair of Liberals who did not know what they were doing. Liberals contesting seats which had not had a Liberal candidate in 1918, because of the Coupon arrangements or the weakness of the organization, lost heavily. A governing party had been reduced, in the electorate's eyes, to a minor party of opposition.

THE RISE OF LABOUR

Liberalism was thus forced to make way for the rising Labour Party.

It was noted above that Labour's performance in 1918 was not spectacular. The Coupon Election had been designed to limit Labour's impact on the electorate, and it succeeded. Labour's subsequent rise can be explained in one of two ways. Some historians prefer to believe that the mere withdrawal of the Liberal Party enabled Labour to take over as the progressive party, appealing to working-class electors. In their view, the war was essential to the rise of Labour, because it killed the principal competitor. Others argue that Labour's main handicap before the war was the prewar franchise, which excluded all women and large numbers of men who might have been expected to support Labour. In the opinion of these historians the 1918 Representation of the People Act created a more 'democratic' franchise which gave the working class the same representation in the electorate as it had in the population as a whole. As a result, they argue, Labour could at last fulfil its potential. The franchise, not the war, allowed Labour to break through.[23]

Few historical arguments are ever settled finally, but recent research points strongly to the war rather than the franchise as the determining factor. The prewar franchise did discriminate against some members of the working class, but it discriminated more harshly against young unmarried men of all classes, and against women, who were of course excluded completely. Moreover, in the 1918 and 1922 elections, which saw Labour rise to an unassailable lead over the Liberals, it can be shown that both women and the newly enfranchised male electors tended towards the Conservatives. As between Labour and Liberal, both of the newly enfranchised groups tended towards the Liberals. The strength of the Labour vote lay in those sections of the working class which were enfranchised before the war: the older, more skilled men who were more likely to be trade unionists. These were the sections of the working class whose political awareness had been consolidated during the war. Increasing trade union membership was only one part of this process, though it was an important one since the unions were the financial and organizational backbone of the party. In industrial areas the habit of collective organization and working-class self-help had been spread beyond the workplace by the circumstances of war. The Glasgow rent-strikes of 1915 were a notorious example of this, but

23 See H. G. C. Matthew, R. I. McKibbin and J.A. Kay, 'The franchise factor in the rise of the Labour Party', *English Historical Review*, vol. 91, no. 361 (1976); Duncan Tanner, 'The parliamentary electoral system, the "Fourth" Reform Act, and the rise of Labour in England and Wales', *Bulletin of the Institute of Historical Research*, vol. 56, no. 134 (1983).

more generally important were the role of the labour movement's own organizations in representing the interests of pensioners and soldiers' dependents, and the party's prominent role in the defence of consumers' interests through the Workers' Emergency National Committee. Sympathy for Labour was built outwards from a core of trade union organization and solidarity. Women and younger men, who lacked established links with the Labour movement, did not at first warm to Labour, and the party's postwar electoral successes were achieved despite the new franchise, not because of it.[24]

A CONSERVATIVE FUTURE

The Conservative Party, appropriately, gets the last word. The 1918 election was a victory for the Conservatives as well as for Lloyd George. They did better than they probably would have done in 1915, and they were undoubtedly the dominant force in the 1919–22 coalition. The year 1918 was the foundation on which their predominance in interwar politics was built. The war had certainly emphasized the values for which Conservatives had traditionally stood, such as patriotism, and some of the more transient Tory policies such as economic protectionism. It had discredited the reputation of the Liberal leadership, which until 1914 had been one of the Liberals' greatest assets. It had allowed Bonar Law, a cautious leader who had had to deal with formidable rivals at the head of the party, to establish his leadership. But it did so by papering over some major cracks. The Tariff Reform crisis, which lasted in the party for nearly ten years up to 1913, had encouraged backbench pressure groups to grow up in the parliamentary party, and created an independent and often cantankerous spirit in local party organizations. The war magnified this effect. Two backbench groups, the Unionist War Committee and the Unionist Business Committee, became vehicles for criticizing the party leadership. The work of candidate reselection, which had started in 1913, brought a number of protectionist businessmen into the parliamentary party in by-elections, and in the 1918 election this trickle naturally became a flood. The new business MPs were inexperienced and difficult to manage, and the party organizers were alarmed that so many should be returned to the 1919 Parliament. Though Bonar Law was a Tariff Reformer, and a former businessman himself, he found it uncomfortable to lead a

24 John Turner, 'Labour and the franchise after 1918', in P. R. Denley and D. I. Hopkin, *History and Computing* (Manchester: Manchester University Press, 1987).

parliamentary party which reminded friends and enemies alike of a particularly narrow-minded Chamber of Commerce. The crudeness of many of the new recruits made it all the more galling that the party was still apparently dependent on Lloyd George for leadership. The old guard of the Tory Party thought he was 'a dirty little rogue'; the new members liked his anti-Bolshevist tirades but were soon impatient with his residual social radicalism, which they neither liked nor understood. Wartime coalitions were on the whole bad for the Conservatives, depriving them of the undisputed dominance which most of them thought they deserved, and depriving many of them of ministerial promotion. Worst of all, the war saddled them with a peacetime coalition which had all the problems and, as time went on, fewer of the justifications of the wartime arrangement. Only by shaking off Lloyd George in 1922 did the Tories come fully into their political inheritance.

By then the shape of postwar politics was becoming clearer. The Conservative Party had resumed its dominance of British politics. Politics in wartime had been driven, at parliamentary level, by the needs and demands of the Conservatives, and it cannot be surprising that the outcome was favourable to them. The war had divided their opponents, substituting a weak newcomer for the robust and confident Liberal Party which had elbowed them aside in 1906. Mass democracy, as embodied in the 1918 Franchise Act, held no terrors for them. Through the effacement of the Liberals, and the hardening of capitalist sympathies within the Conservative Party, the politics of class had come to dominate the party system, and the Conservatives were confident of holding their own in any class war. Labour's reach, for the moment, exceeded its grasp; and in a development which now seems pregnant with significance for the future the Labour Party inherited Liberal strongholds in industrial areas in northern England and, after 1922, in Scotland and Wales, without consolidating its hold on the working class in the south-east or making inroads among Liberal voters in the suburbs. The political pattern of the mid-twentieth century was beginning to emerge in a recognizable form.

Epilogue

JOHN TURNER

No one has attempted in this book to make an ethical judgement on the merits of fighting the First World War, or on its consequences. This is perhaps inevitable in a collective work, but it may not be what every reader expects. Historians now tend to give the war a timid but undeniable endorsement. A recent textbook concludes thus:

> What seems of particular note is the congruity between Haig's affirmation that the issue at stake was 'the safety of our homes and the freedom of mankind' and Massingham's characterization of the conflict as 'a war of defence', a war 'to teach militarism a lesson of restraint'. In short, despite their great differences in background and outlook, each was prepared to proclaim that this was in truth one of freedom's battles.
>
> Perhaps, in so perceiving the conflict, the traditionalist Field-Marshal and the radical journalist were both deluded.
>
> Perhaps, on the other hand, they were not.[1]

From the point of view of a social historian, writing twenty years before:

> ...no one but a romantic reactionary would wish to regret the world which disappeared in the deluge of 1914–1918....Doubtless a new age in Britain would have been ushered in more slowly and more agreeably if there had been no war, if social and political forces, spared its distorting effects, had been left to march more closely in unison. But the war is an historical fact, whose consequences, in the end, can only be presented, not argued over. Its greatest significance is as a revelation, not so much of the folly of statesmen, but of the irrationality and love of violence bedded in human society.[2]

1 Trevor Wilson, *The Myriad Faces of War* (Cambridge: Polity Press, 1986), p. 853.
2 Arthur Marwick, *The Deluge* (London: Macmillan, 1965), p. 314.

Those who approach the war through the studies presented here, and the further reading suggested, will form their own views. They may even find it profitable to argue over the consequences of the war, instead of accepting them as given. But, above all, we hope that these studies of Britain at war will give readers some insight into the complexity of war in the twentieth century: a complexity which seems to the editor, though not necessarily to his fellow-contributors, to defy the optimism of historians who have conscripted the Great War into the onward march of progress.

Military and Naval Chronology of the First World War

(Naval activity in italics)

1914

August

3	Germany declares war on France
4	Britain declares war on Germany
7	British Expeditionary Force begins to land in France
26–29	Russians defeated by Germans at battle of Tannenberg
28	*Battle of Heligoland Bight*

September

5	Britain, France and Russia sign Pact of London
6–9	German advance on Paris halted at Battle of the Marne

October

12 (to 17 November)	German advance on Channel ports halted at First Battle of Ypres
29	Turkey enters the war on the side of the Central Powers

November

1	British troops land in Mesopotamia
	Battle of Coronel

December

8   *Battle of the Falklands*
16   *German battle-cruiser attack on north-
                           east coast towns*

1915

January

24   *Battle of Dogger Bank*

February

4   *German declaration of submarine war
                           zone around United Kingdom (sus-
                           pended 30 August 1915)*
19 (to 19 March)   *Allied naval assault at Dardanelles fails*

March

10   Britain promises Constantinople to Rus-
                           sia at end of war
10–13   Battle of Neuve Chapelle

April

25   Allied troops land at Gallipoli. Italy
                           signs Treaty of London

May

5–6   German breakthrough at Gorlice-Tarnow
9   Battle of Festubert

August

5   Germans occupy Warsaw
6–15   Failure of Suvla Bay operation at
                           Gallipoli

September

23   Bulgaria joins Central Powers, who
                           attack Serbia

October
5   Anglo-French landing at Salonika

December
2   Central Powers occupy Serbia
8 (to 9 January 1916)   Evacuation of Gallipoli

1916

February
21 (to 18 December)   Battle of Verdun

March
29   *Submarine war zone reactivated with
                               some limitations (suspended 20 April)*
29   Fall of Kut-el-Amara

May
31   *Battle of Jutland*

June
4   Arab Revolt begins
4 (to 7   Brusilov offensive on Russian front
September)

July
1 (to 17
November)   Anglo-French offensive on the Somme

August
27   Romania joins the Entente

December
6   Germans occupy Bucharest

1917

February
1   *Completely unrestricted submarine war-
                                fare declared*

March
12   First Russian Revolution

April
6   America enters the war
16–20   Nivelle offensive fails
27   *Convoy system introduced*

July
31 (to 6 November)   Third Battle of Ypres (Passchendaele)

October
24 (to 12 November)   Italians defeated at Caporetto

November
7   Bolshevik Revolution in Russia
20 (to 3 December)   Battle of Cambrai

December
9   British capture Jerusalem
15   Russians sign armistice with Germany

1918

March
3   Treaty of Brest-Litovsk
21 (to 4 April)   Start of German western offensive

May
5   Germans occupy Sebastopol

| 27 (to 3 June) | Battle of the Aisne |

August

| 8 | Second Battle of Amiens. The 'black day' of the German army |

September

15–29	Allied offensive at Salonika forces Bulgaria to sue for peace
18 (to 7 October)	Allied troops on Western Front break through the Hindenburg line
30	British troops occupy Damascus

October

24 (to 4 November)	Italians defeat Austrians at Vittorio Veneto
29	*Mutinies in German High Seas Fleet*
30	Turkey signs armistice

November

3	Austria signs armistice
11	Germany signs armistice
21	*German High Seas Fleet interned at Scapa Flow*

Suggested Reading

Of the making of books about the First World War there is no ending. A bibliography of books on the war written in English, published in 1979 and manifestly incomplete even then, contained nearly 5,800 entries. (A. G. S. Enser, *A Subject Bibliography of the First World War: Books in English 1914–1978*, London: Andre Deutsch, 1979.) What follows is therefore a selection made by the contributors, to indicate possible directions of exploration. It includes both classic accounts, often quite old, and very recent works, and where appropriate it guides the reader to specialized articles in periodicals.

GENERAL

A bold attempt at a general history of Britain during the war has recently been made by Trevor Wilson in *The Myriad Faces of War* (Cambridge: Polity Press, 1986), a synthesis of recent writing on the war accompanied by imaginative use of unpublished diaries, correspondence and recollections of ordinary people caught up in the struggle both in the forces and on the Home Front. One could scarcely imagine a greater contrast than with the still useful account of the course of the fighting in C. R. F. M. Cruttwell, *A History of the Great War* (Oxford: Clarendon Press, 1934). Somewhere between the two is Sir Llewellyn Woodward, *Great Britain and the War of 1914-18* (London: Methuen, 1967).

STRATEGY AND WAR AIMS

The best introduction to the development of British strategy and war aims during the First World War remains Paul Guinn, *British Strategy and Politics 1914 to 1918* (Oxford: Clarendon Press, 1965). However, since its publication the public records for the whole of the war together with a great many collections of private papers have become available to historians and Guinn's conclusions have been subject both to modification and to amplification. Paul M. Kennedy, *The Rise of the Anglo-German Antagonism 1860–1914* (London: Allen & Unwin, 1980) investigates Anglo-German relations before 1914, and Zara S. Steiner, *Britain and the Origins of the First World War* (London: Macmillan, 1977), explains why Britain entered the war. David French, *British Economic and Strategic Planning, 1905–1915* (London: Allen & Unwin, 1982) brings together some of the literature on Britain's prewar military planning and looks at how 'business as usual' evolved in the opening months of the war.

V. H. Rothwell, *British War Aims and Peace Diplomacy, 1914–1918* (Oxford: Clarendon Press, 1971), is a detailed introduction to the debate on British war aims within the policy-making elite. It concentrates on the last two years of the war. David French, *British Strategy and War Aims, 1914–1916* (London/Boston Mass.: Allen & Unwin, 1986) has attempted to fill the gap for 1914–16. The crucial role played by Russia in shaping British policy has been examined by Keith Neilson, *Strategy and Supply: The Anglo-Russian Alliance, 1914–1917* (London: Allen & Unwin, 1984). The evolution of British policy towards Austria-Hungary can be traced in W. B. Fest, *Peace or Partition: The Habsburg Monarchy and British Policy, 1914–1918* (London: George Prior, 1978), and Kenneth J. Calder, *Britain and the Origins of the New Europe, 1914–1918* (Cambridge: Cambridge University Press, 1976). Lorna S. Jaffe, *The Decision to Disarm Germany: British Policy Towards Postwar German Disarmament, 1914–1918* (London: Allen & Unwin, 1985), is an excellent discussion of what the British meant by 'Prussian militarism' and George W. Egerton, *Great Britain and the Creation of the League of Nations: Strategy, Politics and International Organisation, 1914–1919* (London: Scolar Press, 1979), shows to what extent President Wilson was able to influence British attitudes on this crucial issue. Kathleen Burk, *Britain, America and the Sinews of War, 1914–1918* (London: Allen & Unwin, 1985) charts Britain's growing economic dependence on the United States of America.

John Gooch, 'Soldiers, strategy and war aims in Britain 1914–1918', in B. Hunt and A. Preston (eds), *War Aims and Strategic Policy in the Great War* (London: Croom Helm, 1977) and David Woodward, *Lloyd George and the Generals* (London: Associated University Press, 1983), are important sources for the development of civil–military relations. For the soldiers they can be supplemented by a clutch of studies: including *The Private Papers of Douglas Haig, 1914–1918*, ed. Robert Blake (London: Eyre & Spottiswoode, 1952); John Terraine, *Douglas Haig: The Educated Soldier* (London: Hutchinson, 1963); Victor Bonham-Carter, *Soldier True: The Life and Times of Field-Marshal Sir William Robertson, 1860–1933* (London: Muller, 1963); and Richard Holmes, *The Little Field-Marshal: Sir John French* (London: Cape, 1981). The careers of the two wartime prime ministers have been examined by Roy Jenkins, *Asquith* (London: Collins, 1964) and John Grigg, *Lloyd George: From Peace to War, 1912–1916* (London: Methuen, 1985). Kitchener's career has most recently been re-examined by T. Royle, *The Kitchener Enigma* (London: Michael Joseph, 1985).

THE WAR AND THE BRITISH EMPIRE

A contemporary account of *The Empire at War* was edited by a former

Colonial Office official, Sir Charles Lucas in 5 volumes (London: Oxford University Press for the Royal Colonial Institute, 1921–6). *The Cambridge History of the British Empire*, Vol. 3 (Cambridge: Cambridge University Pres, 1959), contains substantial chapters by C. E. Carrington on 'The Empire at war, 1914–1918' (pp. 605–44) and K. C. Wheare on 'The Empire and the peace treaties, 1918–1921' (pp. 645–66). Max Beloff, *Imperial Sunset*, Vol. 1, *Britain's Liberal Empire, 1897–1921* (London: Methuen, 1969), and Nicholas Mansergh, *The Commonwealth Experience*, Vol. 1, 2nd edn (London: Macmillan, 1982), provide authoritative introductions to the problems of empire in war and peace, while J. Gallagher's lectures, *The Decline, Revival and Fall of the British Empire* (Cambridge: Cambridge University Press, 1981), are essential reading on the twentieth-century Empire.

The Dominions and Commonwealth dimension of the war and postwar periods have been the subject of a number of classic studies, notably Robert McGregor Dawson (ed.), *The Development of Dominion Status, 1900–1936* (London: Oxford University Press, 1937), which contains a collection of constitutional documents, and W. K. Hancock, *Survey of British Commonwealth Affairs*, Vol. 1, *Problems of Nationality, 1918–1936* (London: Oxford University Press for the Royal Institute of International Affairs, 1937) and Vol. 2, Pt 1, *Problems of Economic Policy, 1918–1939* (1940). The Commonwealth in the interwar years has been examined more recently by R. F. Holland, *Britain and the Commonwealth Alliance, 1918–1939* (London: Macmillan, 1981).

For the war in Africa, see W. Roger Louis, *Great Britain and Germany's Lost Colonies, 1914–1919* (Oxford: Clarendon Press, 1967), and David Killingray, 'Repercussions of World War I in the Gold Coast', *Journal of African History*, vol. 19, no 1 (1978), pp. 39–59. For changes in Britain's relationship with India, see P. G. Robb, *The Government of India and Reform, 1916–21* (London: Oxford University Press, 1976), and B. R. Tomlinson, *The Political Economy of the Raj, 1914–47: The Economics of Decolonization* (London: Macmillan, 1979). J. G. Darwin has studied Britain's extended empire in the Middle East in *Britain, Egypt and the Middle East: Imperial Policy in the Aftermath of War, 1918–1922* (London: Macmillan, 1981), and his article 'Imperialism in decline? Tendencies in British imperial policy between the wars', *Historical Journal*, vol. 23, no. 3 (1980), pp. 657–79, is an assessment of the 'official mind' of British imperialism after the Great War. The military strains experienced in defending the postwar Empire are dealt with by Keith Jeffery, *The British Army and the Crisis of Empire, 1918–22* (Manchester: Manchester University Press, 1984), and Anthony Clayton, *The British Empire as a Superpower, 1919–39* (London: Macmillan, 1986).

Particular aspects of the Empire at war have been treated in the following articles published in the *Journal of Imperial and Commonwealth History*: N. G. Garson, 'South Africa and World War I', vol. 8 no. 1 (October, 1979), pp. 68–85; Jeffrey Greenhut, 'The imperial reserve: the Indian Corps on the Western Front, 1914–15', vol. 12, no. 1 (October 1983); pp. 54–73; John S. Galbraith, 'British war aims in World War I: a commentary on "statesmanship" ', vol. 13, no. 1 (October 1984), pp. 25–45; Gregory Martin, 'The influence of racial attitudes on British policy towards India during the First World War', vol. 14, no. 2 (January 1986), pp. 91–113.

THE WAR AT SEA

There is no reliable shorter substitute for A. J. Marder, *From the Dreadnought to Scapa Flow*, 5 vols (London: Oxford University Press, 1961–70). Vol. 3 deals with Jutland; Vol. 5 has a masterly overview of the whole war and a comprehensive bibliography. Sir Llewellyn Woodward, *Great Britain and the War of 1914–18* (London: Methuen, 1967), puts the naval operations within the general pattern of the war. The most important biographies are: A. Temple-Patterson, *Jellicoe: A Biography* (London: Macmillan, 1969), and S. W. Roskill, *Admiral of the Fleet Earl Beatty* (London: Collins, 1981). The theories of maritime strategy are well summarized in D. M. Schurman, *The Education of a Navy: The Development of British Naval Strategic Thought, 1867–1914* (London: Cassell, 1965). The contribution of naval intelligence is expertly described in P. Beesly, *Room 40: British Naval Intelligence, 1914–18* (London: Hamish Hamilton, 1982). Marder, *From Dreadnought to Scapa Flow*, Vol. 5, Part 3, *The Human Factor*, contrasts British and German leadership and morale. Henry Baynham, *Men from the Dreadnoughts* (London: Hutchinson, 1976), consists of personal lower-deck reminiscences and is well illustrated. Anthony Carew, *The Lower Deck of the Royal Navy, 1900–1939: The Invergordon Mutiny in Perspective* (Manchester: Manchester University Press, 1981), analyses the pre-1914 reforms. The social structure and ethos of the German navy are authoritatively analysed in Holger M. Herwig, *The German Naval Officer Corps: A Social and Political History, 1890–1918* (Oxford: Clarendon Press, 1973).

MEN, MUNITIONS AND MONEY

Britain's economic experience during the war, as distinct from the war's consequences, has not received much attention. Sidney Pollard's *The Development of the British Economy 1914–1980*, 3rd edn (London: Edward Arnold, 1983), is the best introduction. A great deal about economic policy was published in the 1920s in the Carnegie Histories, notably E. M. H. Lloyd *Experiments in State Control* (London: Oxford University Press, 1924); W. H. Beveridge *British Food Control* (London: Oxford University Press, 1928), and the very undistinguished T. H. Middleton *Food Production in War* (London: Oxford University Press, 1923). Some of these volumes have extensive accounts of economic activity as well, as does the official but almost unobtainable *History of the Ministry of Munitions*, 8 Vols (London: HMSO, 1922). Mostly written by temporary or permanent civil servants, all these studies have to be complimented by more detached recent work. Kathleen Burk (ed.), *War and the State* (London: Allen & Unwin, 1982) contains relevant articles by José Harris (on food control), Rodney Lowe (on labour) and Burk herself (on the Treasury and finance). Kathleen Burk, *Britain, America and the Sinews of War, 1914–1918*, cited above under war aims, deals with external financing; for internal taxation one must go back to E. V. Morgan, *Studies in British Financial Policy, 1914–1925* (London: Macmillan, 1952).

Intervention in industry is dealt with in parts of J. M. Winter (ed.), *War and Economic Development* (Cambridge: Cambridge University Press, 1975), and in various industrial and business histories such as T. H. Burnham and G. O. Hoskins, *Iron and Steel in Britain, 1870–1930* (London: Allen & Unwin, 1943). An interesting sidelight is shed by R. P. T. Davenport-Hines, *Dudley Docker. The life and times of a trade warrior*, (Cambridge: Cambridge University Press, 1985)

John Terraine, *White Heat: The New Warfare, 1914–1918* (London: Sidgwick & Jackson, 1982), is illuminating on the interaction between tactics, military technology and industrial effort, while Gerd Hardach, *The First World War* (London: Allen Lane, 1977), gives an international view of wartime economic history. For the economic consequences of the war, the best concise accounts are still A. L. Bowley, *The Economic Consequences of the Great War* (London: Thornton, Butterworth, 1930) and Alan S. Milward, *The Economic Consequences of the Two World Wars for Britain* (London: Macmillan, 1970).

THE BRITISH POPULATION AT WAR

Although it is one of the oldest social histories of the First World War, Arthur Marwick's *The Deluge* (London: Macmillan, 1965; 2nd edn, 1973) remains the most comprehensive – and readable – account of the general impact of the conflict, written by a historian who pioneered research into the effects of war on social change. Of the more recent major studies of social history, J. M. Winter, *The Great War and the British People* (London: Macmillan, 1986), is principally concerned with the demographic impact of war. The author analyses the reasons for an evident improvement in civilian health, pressing home the argument he first put forward in 'The impact of the First World War on civilian health in Britain', *Economic History Review*, 2nd ser., vol. 30, no. 3 (1977), pp. 489–504. The book is based on a mass of detailed statistical evidence, and the inquiry is broadened to examine the notion of a 'lost generation' which resulted from the war – as well as explaining why living standards rose during the conflict. It is a seminal work which will inspire many further detailed studies. New research, building on the same foundation but emphasizing some of the less desirable consequences of the war, is for example reported in Linda Bryden, 'The First World War: healthy or hungry', *History Workshop*, no. 24 (Autumn 1987), pp. 141–57. Bernard Waites has recently published *A Class Society at War: England, 1914–1918* (Leamington Spa: Berg Publishers, 1987), which sets out the result of his work on society in the war first expounded in 'The effect of the First World War on class and status in England, 1919–20', *Journal of Contemporary History*, vol. 2, no. 1 (1976), pp. 27–48. Dr Waites is interested in the relationship between social theory – notably on questions of class – and historical evidence. His work examines the impact of war on the distribution of wealth, on social structure and on notions of class, class consciousness and political attitudes.

The study of industrial relations during the war was brought to life by James Hinton in *The First Shop Stewards' Movement* (London: Allen & Unwin, 1973). Following the work of B. Pribicevic, *The Shop Stewards' Movement and Workers' Control 1910–22* (Oxford: Blackwell, 1959), Hinton examined the rising incidence of industrial militancy in munitions during the war, the revolutionary potential of the shop stewards' movement and how state and employers managed to contain the threat. This work has been criticized by Ian McLean in *The Legend of Red Clydeside* (Edinburgh: John Macdonald, 1983), which calls into question the revolutionary and progressive nature of the workers' aims; and by Alastair Reid in 'Dilution, trade unionism and the state in Britain during the First World War' in S. Tolliday and J. Zeitlin, *Shop Floor Bargaining and the State* (Cambridge: Cambridge University Press, 1985). Reid in particular emphasizes how the political power of the working class, far from being reduced by state intervention, was consolidated and enhanced by wartime developments. A comprehensive overview of industrial relations and wage bargaining during the war can be found in C. J. Wrigley, 'The First World War and state intervention in industrial relations, 1914-1918', in C.J. Wrigley, *A History of British Industrial Relations*, vol. 2 (Hassocks: Harvester, 1987).

Studies of women during the war have generated much heat but less light: the most comprehensive work is still Arthur Marwick, *Women at War, 1914–1918* (London: Croom Helm, 1977), a highly descriptive account of the changes in women's lives brought about by the war, amply illustrated. At the time of going to press, however, Gail Braybon and Penny Summerfield, *Out of the Cage* (London: Pandora, 1987) awaited publication and may well merit serious attention.

THE BRITISH ARMY

The themes raised in this essay are discussed at greater length in Ian F. W. Beckett and Keith Simpson (eds), *A Nation in Arms: A Social Study of the British Army in the First World War* (Manchester: Manchester University Press, 1985), which contains a full bibliography in addition to individual essay bibliographies and notes. Similarly, Edward Spiers, *The Army and Society, 1815–1914* (London: Longman, 1980), provides a full bibliography and additional information on the prewar army.

For recruitment and a revision of the 'rush to the colours', see J.J. Becker, *1914: Comment les francais sont entrés dans la guerre* (Paris: Presses de la Fondation Nationale des Sciences Politiques, 1977), and L. L. Farrar, 'Reluctant warriors: public opinion during the July crisis', *Eastern European Quarterly*, vol. 16, no.4 (1982), pp. 417–46. Individual studies of recruitment in particular areas can be found in M. D. Blanch, 'Nation, Empire and the Birmingham working class, 1899–1914', unpublished PhD thesis, Birmingham University, 1975, fos 341–67; Clive Hughes, 'Army recruitment in Gwynedd, 1914–1916', unpublished MA thesis, University of Wales, 1983, pp. 336–9; Patricia Morris, 'Leeds and the amateur military tradition: the Leeds Rifles and their antecedents, 1859–1918', unpublished PhD thesis, Leeds University, 1983, fos 309–61; and J. M. Osborne, *The Voluntary Recruiting Movement in Britain, 1914–1916* (New York/London: Garland, 1982), which focuses on Bristol.

In addition to Peter Dewey's important article, 'Military recruiting and the British labour force during the First World War', *Historical Journal*, vol. 27, no. 1 (1984), and J. M. Winter's essay, 'Britain's lost generation of the First World War', *Population Studies*, vol. 31, no. 3 (1977), attention should also be directed at Winter's other articles: 'Some aspects of the demographic consequences of the First World War in Britain', *Population Studies*, vol. 30, no. 3 (1976), pp. 539–52; and 'Military fitness and civilian health in Britain during the First World War', *Journal of Contemporary History*, vol. 15, no. 2 (1980), pp. 211-44. Much of this material is reproduced in his *The Great War and the British People* (London: Macmillan, 1985).

For aspects of the idea of a 'war generation', see E. J. Leed, 'Class and disillusionment in World War One', *Journal of Modern History*, vol. 50, no. 4 (1978), pp. 680–99; E. J. Leed, *No Man's Land* (Cambridge: Cambridge University Press, 1979); R. Wohl, *The Generation of 1914* (London: Weidenfeld & Nicolson, 1980); and Richard Bessel and David Englander, 'Up from the trenches: some recent writing on the soldiers of the Great War', *European Studies Review*, vol. 11, no. 3 (1981), pp. 387–95. Ex-servicemen are dealt with in S. R. Ward, 'Intelligence surveillance of British ex-servicemen, 1918–1920', *Historical Journal*, vol. 16, no. 1 (1973), pp. 179–88; S. R. Ward, 'Great Britain', in S. R. Ward (ed.), *The War Generation* (Port Washington, NY: Kennikat Press, 1975), pp. 10–37; and David Englander and James Osborne, 'Jack, Tommy and Henry Dubb: the armed forces and the working class', *Historical Journal*, vol. 21, no. 3 (1978), pp. 593–621. The last throws some light upon demobilization disturbances, as does Andrew Rothstein, *The Soldiers' Strikes of 1919* (London: Macmillan, 1980).

The particular question of manpower distribution between the army and other sectors is the theme of D. R. Woodward, 'Did Lloyd George starve the British army of men prior to the German offensive of 21 March 1918?', *Historical Journal*, vol. 27, no. 1 (1984), pp. 241–52; D. R. Woodward, *Lloyd George and the Generals* (London/Toronto: Associated University Presses, 1983); F. W. Perry, 'Manpower and organizational problems in the expansion of the British and Commonwealth armies during the two world wars', unpublished PhD thesis, London University, 1982, fos 14–80; and Keith Grieves, 'The British government's political and administrative response to the manpower problem in the First World War', unpublished PhD thesis, Manchester University, 1984.

For the working of conscription, in terms of conscientious objectors, see John Rae, *Conscience and Politics* (London: Oxford University Press, 1970); and T. C. Kennedy, *The Hound of Conscience* (Fayetteville, Ark.:

University of Arkansas Press, 1981).

For case studies of individual components of the British army and individual battalions, see the essays by Beckett and Hughes in Ian Beckett and Keith Simpson, *A Nation in Arms*, which deal with the Buckinghamshire battalions of the Territorial Force and the 113th Brigade of the New Army respectively (Ian Beckett, 'The Territorial Force', pp. 127–64, and Clive Hughes, 'The New Armies', pp. 99–126). Ian Beckett has also focused on the 48th Division in 'The Territorial Force in the Great War', in Peter Liddle (ed.), *Home Fires and Foreign Fields* (London: Brasseys, 1985), pp. 21–38. Apart from G. D. Sheffield's study of the 22nd Royal Fusiliers, 'The effect of war service on the 22nd Battalion, Royal Fusiliers (Kensingtons), 1914–1918, with special reference to morale, discipline and the officer/man relationship', unpublished MA thesis, Leeds University, 1984, there is also Patricia Morris's study of the Leeds Rifles. Peter Simkins has also touched on the New Armies in his 'Kitchener and the expansion of the army', in I. F. W. Beckett and John Gooch (eds), *Politicians and Defence* (Manchester: Manchester University Press, 1981), pp. 87–109. Aspects of the varied experience of soldiers are also brought out in Keith Simpson, 'The British soldier on the Western Front', in Liddle, *Home Fires and Foreign Fields*, pp. 135–58.

On officers and the wartime military mind, see Keith Simpson's essay in *Nation in Arms* but also T. H. E. Travers, 'The offensive and the problem of innovation in British militray thought, 1870–1915', *Journal of Contemporary History*, vol. 13, no. 3 (1978), 531–53; his 'The hidden structural problem in the British officer corps, 1900–1918', *Journal of Contemporary History*, vol. 17, no. 3 (1982), pp. 523–44; and also his 'Learning and decision-making on the Western Front: the British example, 1915–1916', *Canadian Journal of History*, April 1983, pp 87–97.

POLITICS

Like the history of strategy, the history of wartime politics has suffered from the eagerness of the main participants to get their stories out. Winston Churchill's *The World Crisis* (London: Thornton Butterworth, 1923–31) and David Lloyd George, *War Memoirs*, 2 vol. edn (London: Odhams, 1938) are the most interesting because of their authors, and because they reprint a great deal of original material, but they lack even the pretence of political objectivity. Churchill's account is examined by Robin Prior in *Churchill's 'World Crisis' as History* (London: Croom Helm, 1983)

Early attempts to write a political history of the war were pre-empted by Lord Beaverbrook in *Politicians and the War* (London: Butterworth, 1928–1932) and *Men and Power* (London: Hutchinson, 1956). What Beaverbrook did not see through the eyes of his patron Bonar Law, he saw in the Lloyd George Papers, which he had bought when he wrote *Men and Power*. He also corresponded with many active politicians. His work is therefore in part an 'inside story' of Cabinet intrigue, but he was poorly informed about the workings of Parliament and utterly ignorant about popular political attitudes. His vivid narrative should therefore be complemented by the sober scholarship of Cameron Hazlehurst, *Politicians at War* (London: Jonathan Cape, 1971), which deals with the Liberal Cabinet at war. Trevor Wilson, *The Downfall of the Liberal Party* (London: Collins, 1966), takes a broad sweep, but is obviously prejudiced against Lloyd George. Michael Bentley, *The Liberal Mind* (Cambridge: Cambridge University Press, 1977), though hard going, is a more balanced analysis of Liberal difficulties. There is no study of the Asquith coalition to correspond to Hazlehurst: John Turner's forthcoming *British Politics and the Crisis of War* examines the tribulations of the Lloyd George coalition from 1916 to 1918. C. J. Wrigley, in *David Lloyd George and the British Labour Movement* (Hassocks: Harvester Press, 1976), has important material on the Labour Party as well as on the trade union movement. Kenneth O. Morgan, *Consensus and Disunity: The Lloyd George Coalition Government 1918–1922* (Oxford: Clarendon Press, 1979) gives an account of immediate postwar politics which is broadly sympathetic to Lloyd George.

Some interesting and useful primary sources for Westminster politics are now available in print: Edward David (ed), *Inside Asquith's Cabinet: From the Diaries of Charles Hobhouse* (London: John Murray, 1977); A. J. P. Taylor (ed.), *Lloyd George: A Diary by Frances Stevenson* (London: Hutchinson, 1971); John Ramsden (ed.) *Real Old Tory Politics: The Political Diaries of Robert Sanders, Lord Bayford* (London: Historians' Press, 1984).

On electoral politics Martin Pugh, *Electoral Reform in War and Peace, 1906–1918* (London: Routledge & Kegan Paul, 1978) gives a good account of the making of the 1918 Representation of the People Act. H. G. C. Matthew, R. I. McKibbin, and J. A. Kay, in 'The franchise factor and the rise of the Labour Party', *English Historical Review*, vol. 91, no. 361 (1976), are strongly opposed to the idea that the war contributed much to Labour's growth. Michael Hart 'The Liberals, the war and the franchise', *English Historical Review*, vol. 97, no. 385 (1982), puts the opposite case. R. I. McKibbin *The Evolution of the Labour Party 1910–1924* (Oxford: Clarendon Press, 1974), gives a cogent account of Labour's organizational development.

The war's effect on political ideas is explored in Peter Clarke, *Liberals and Social Democrats* (Cambridge: Cambridge University Press, 1978); and in J. M. Winter, *Socialism and the Challenge of War* (Cambridge: Cambridge University Press, 1974). Conservatives did not go in for ideeas as such, but the thinking of some reflective Conservatives can be examined in George Boyce, *The Crisis of British Unionism: The Domestic Political Papers of the Second Earl of Selborne* (London: Historians' Press, 1987). Jo Vellacott, 'Feminist consciousness and the First World War', *History Workshop*, no. 23 (Spring 1987) is a sketchy but interesting account of the interaction between feminism, socialism and pacifism during the war. Fuller treatment of pacifism as an idea is found in Martin Ceadel, *Pacifism in Britain 1914–1945: the defining of a faith* (Oxford: Clarendon Press, 1980).

Notes on the Contributors

Ian Beckett was educated at Lancaster University and King's College, London, where he took his PhD in the Department of War Studies. He taught contemporary history at the University of Salford before joining the academic staff of the Royal Military Academy, Sandhurst, where he has been senior lecturer in war studies since 1979. He has written extensively on the armed forces and society, most recently *The Army and the Curragh Incident, 1914* (London: Bodley Head, 1986) and (as editor with Keith Simpson) *A Nation in Arms: A Social Study of the British Army in the First World War* (Manchester: Manchester University Press, 1985). He is general editor of Manchester University Press's new series 'War, Armed Forces and Society'.

Peter Dewey was educated at the universities of Exeter and Reading. He is a lecturer in economic history at Royal Holloway and Bedford New College. He won the T. S. Ashton Prize in 1975 for a study of the agricultural labour force in the First World War, and the Royal Historical Society's Alexander Prize in 1979 for a study of food production in wartime. He contributes regularly to scholarly journals and is now working on a major study of British agriculture in the First World War.

David French is a lecturer in history at University College, London. He was educated at York University and King's College, London, where he took his PhD in the Department of War Studies. He taught at the Polytechnic of North London, Newcastle University, and Heriot-Watt University before taking up his present post. He has written *British Economic and Strategic Planning, 1905–1915* (London: Allen & Unwin, 1982) and *British Strategy and War Aims, 1914–1916* (London: Allen & Unwin, 1986), and is now working on a study of British strategy under the Lloyd George coalition.

Bryan Ranft was professor and head of the Department of History and International Affairs at the Royal Naval College, Greenwich, from 1966 to 1977, and a visiting professor and senior research fellow in the Department of War Studies, King's College, London, from 1970 to 1982. He is best known for his extensive writings on the British navy, but he has also published *The Sea in Soviet Strategy*

(London: Macmillan, 1983) with Geoffrey Till, and most recently has edited *Ironclad to Trident: 100 Years of Defence Commentary* (London: Brassey, 1987). He is now completing an edition of Admiral Beatty's papers for the Navy Records Society.

A. J. Stockwell was educated at St John's College, Cambridge, and the School of Oriental and African Studies, London, and is now a senior lecturer in the Department of History at Royal Holloway and Bedford New College. He specializes in imperial history and the recent history of South-East Asia, and his publications include *British Policy and Malay Politics during the Malayan Union Experiment, 1942–1948* (Kuala Lumpur: Malaysian Branch of the Royal Asiatic Society, 1979) and (with A. N. Porter), *British Imperial Policy and Decolonization, 1938–64*, vol. 1 (London; Macmillan, 1987) and vol. 2 (forthcoming).

John Turner is a lecturer in history at Royal Holloway and Bedford New College. Educated at Worcester College, Oxford, and Yale University, he was a research fellow of Peterhouse, Cambridge, and taught at the Middlesex and City of London Polytechnics before joining the Department of History of Bedford College, London, in 1977. He has published *Lloyd George's Secretariat* (Cambridge: Cambridge University Press, 1980) and edited *Businessmen and Politics* (London: Heinemann Educational Books, 1984). His study of the politics of the Lloyd George coalition is forthcoming from Yale University Press, and he is now working on a biography of Harold Macmillan.

Noel Whiteside was educated at Liverpool University. After taking her doctorate she worked as an assistant keeper at the Public Record Office and subsequently as a research fellow at the Centre for Social History, University of Warwick, before joining Bristol University's Department of Social Administration as a lecturer in 1978. She has published *Casual Labour: the Unemployment Question and the Port Transport Industry, 1880–1970* (Oxford: Oxford University Press, 1980), with Dr G. A., Phillips, and her *Unemployment, the Social Problem* is to be published by Faber & Faber. Her research is focused on labour and labour market policies over the last hundred years, and she has published articles in many leading journals.

Index